Why I am Still an Anglican

To Judy

Wishing you a very happy
next decade with much
fulfilment and joy!
Thank you for all you
contribute to R.S. at Hampton.

Best wishes,

Chris Cullen

2 June 2007

For my parents

Why I am Still an Anglican

Essays and Conversations

Edited by
CAROLINE CHARTRES

continuum

CONTINUUM

The Tower Building,
11 York Road,
London SE1 7NX

80 Maiden Lane,
Suite 704,
New York
NY 10038

www.continuumbooks.com

Introduction, this collection and interviews copyright © Caroline Chartres, 2006
Individual contributions copyright © the contributors, 2006
Dr John Stott's chapter is abridged and adapted from his contribution to *Hope for the Church of England?* edited by Gavin Reid (Kingsway Publications, 1986) and is used with permission.
The extracts from 'Balance' and 'In Church' by R.S. Thomas © Kunjana Thomas, 2001), quoted by Frank Field, are reprinted with permission.

First published 2006
Reprinted 2006

British Library Cataloguing in Publication Data
A catalogue record for this book is available from the British Library.

ISBN 10: 0-8264-8143-4 (hb)
ISBN 13: 978-0-8264-8143-6 (hb)
ISBN 10: 0-8264-8312- (pb)
ISBN 13: 978-0-8264-8312-6 (pb)

Typeset by BookEns Ltd, Royston, Herts
Printed and bound in Great Britain by
MPG Books Ltd, Bodmin, Cornwall

Contents

Contents

Acknowledgements

Thanks to Carolyn Armitage, Commissioning Editor, and her colleagues at Continuum, whose idea this was; to all the contributors for their willingness to take part (and not least for accommodating my erratic timetable); to our children for their remarkable love and forbearance and above all to my Beloved, who bears no responsibility for the contents of this book but is at least part of the reason Why I am Still an Anglican.

Introduction

I am a cradle Anglican. 'Church', in its middle-of-the-road Anglican manifestation, was part of the fabric of my childhood. As a teenager, I played the organ (and discovered that you didn't have to be particularly talented to be in demand for services). I could never afford to rebel against going to church – it was my principal source of income.

I went to a school that had been founded for clergy orphans (which I wasn't), where we learned – and had to recite – the Prayer Book collect every Saturday morning, while we were ostensibly doing our mending. (A more lasting legacy than the memory of the collects is a reluctance on my part to do any darning.)

Every now and then, the routine of formal chapel services would be interrupted by an informal communion service in the Upper (Common) Room. Wafers and wine gave way to cubes of Hovis on plastic plates and a goblet of Ribena. We sat in a circle on cushions or on the floor and hoped not to be the ones who had to share the Peace with our Headmistress. She was a good and godly person who would clasp your hand firmly between hers and look you intently in the eye as she said earnestly: 'The peace of the Lord be always with you, Caroline.' Eye-contact would fail and my voice would tail off in embarrassment before I'd finished saying, 'And also with you, er, Miss, er ...'

Her favourite service was Compline (which I learned was not a foul-tasting though nutritious drink for invalids), and her favourite prayer the passage from St Paul that begins, 'Now unto Him that is able to do exceeding abundantly, above all that we ask or think ...' I discovered that my own favourite service was Evensong. On wet winter Sunday evenings, nothing appealed less than going out from a warm fireside to play the organ in a dark church – but it converted me every time. Twenty-six years ago and 12,000 miles away, I found myself outside Christchurch Cathedral in New Zealand as Evensong was about to begin, and knew I was at home.

There were contrasting experiences also, Anglican and other: a period of running the Christian Union (despite my evident lack of CU credentials or temperament); a Latin Mass, celebrated by a French priest with a speech impediment, which was almost entirely incomprehensible but one of the most profoundly worshipful experiences I have ever had. And years of running Sunday schools (for adults, as well as children) helped to plug some of the gaps in my own knowledge and required me to think more critically about the inheritance of the faith I was trying to pass on.

So my experience of the Church of England was timeless, comforting and comfortable, rather than cutting-edge: it seemed generous, capacious and undemanding. I had a strong sense of God, was Trinitarian by instinct and Anglican in my tastes and lack of fervour, but beyond that gave remarkably little thought to the implications of my Church allegiance. At school, I was envious of my Roman Catholic friends: at least they knew what they were supposed to believe. Even if they didn't agree with their

2

Church's teachings (on birth control, say, or euthanasia, or abortion), it gave them something to kick against, to help to define their own views.

I still admire that but in the meantime, like others in this book, I've been converted to Anglicanism from within. Nothing has done more to strengthen my own faith and my convictions about God than the experience of being a parent and I see in the Church of England (at its best) the best sort of parenting. I've come to value the breadth and the trust of a church that gives me the freedom, within a framework, to make my own judgements; that says that all are welcome to share in its hospitality.

I've also seen something of the breadth and energy of the Anglican Church, especially in London: the work being done across social divides and barriers of race or income. This is not the popular image of the Church of England. Once it was more commonly portrayed as an object of fun or pity, an anachronism or an irrelevance. People were assumed to be Anglican by default, because they weren't anything more interesting, or perhaps because faith didn't matter very much to them anyway.

Today, apathy has been superseded by schism (or the threat of it). Hardly a day passes without reports of the latest disagreement to tear at the heart of the Anglican Communion. We appear to have sex on the brain (which, as the old joke goes, is a very uncomfortable place to have it). We are reportedly riven with factions, for or against gay priests, or women bishops, or civil partnerships, and our internal debates are sometimes characterized by a marked lack of charity.

It was famously said of the eighteenth-century Bishop Warburton that, had he been aboard Noah's Ark, he would have occupied 'a small corner of rationality, as much appalled by the stench within as by the tempest without'. It's easy to suppose that plenty of people today might feel rather the same way about the Church of England.

Ask a cross-section of them, therefore, to explain (for the purposes of this book) why they are still Anglicans, and it might be thought prudent to rush into print very quickly, before they can change their minds. The underlying assumption is that – if indeed they are still Anglican – they might not be for very much longer. Surely they must soon tire of the bickering, be driven out by dissent, or simply disappear out of boredom or weariness?

Put this suggestion to the individuals in question, however, and you discover that nothing could be further from the truth. They may dissent from some of the Church's decisions, regret the current disagreements, be infuriated by the General Synod, or woolly bishops, or troublesome priests, but leaving the Church is simply not an option. They are not just steadfast, but unexpectedly passionate.

This is surprising. Another old joke defines an Anglican as someone who can believe anything they want, as long as they don't believe it too strongly. More recently, Roger Scruton wrote:

> The truth about the Anglican Church is simple: it is a longstanding pact between God and England, where-by our country, its language and its manners are brought within the Christian fold, but without demanding anything embarrassing by way of belief, ritual or devotion.[1]

That makes Anglicanism hard to pin down. All Christian churches teach that we are persons in communion and bring people together to learn to relate to God, to each other and to the world around us. By talking (most of the chapters are based on interviews) to Anglicans whose ages span half a century and whose experiences embrace half the globe, this book seeks to capture something of the distinctive but elusive flavour of the Church of England.

Despite the widely differing ages, backgrounds and perspectives of the contributors, some common themes emerge: a dislike of labels ('evangelical', 'liberal', 'charismatic', etc.); an enthusiasm for the parish system and for Prayer Book Evensong (whether under turning fans in the tropical heat or in Sir Christopher Wren's great masterpiece at the heart of London); an appreciation, rather than resentment, of a church that is broad enough to contain those of opposing views.

A church that has grown through turbulent times, holding in tension the historic inheritance of Catholicism with the insights of the Reformation and seeking to follow a *via media*, is always going to be open to charges of fence-sitting. But the Church of England does reflect, in a profound way, the character and temperament of the English people. It knows that, told what to do, we become counter-suggestible – so it requires us to think for ourselves (and leaves open the possibility that we won't think at all). It embraces Anglo-Catholics, middle-of-the-road don't-knows and neo-Puritans, which – if we could only cease our (below-the-)navel-gazing and look together in the same direction – would still be an enormous strength.

What follows is not a profound theological tome (although it begins with a distinguished theologian putting the Church of England into its historical and theological context), nor an attempt to plaster over the cracks that are currently only too visible within the Anglican Communion. Rather, it is a personal, partial and affectionate (though by no means uncritical) glimpse of the Anglican Church, whose diversity should still – most of the time – be a cause for celebration.

Caroline Chartres

NOTE

1. *Country Life*, 9 June 2005.

1

Pursuing Truth and Unity

John Stott *became Rector Emeritus of London's famous All Souls Church, Langham Place in 1975, after 25 years of distinguished service as Rector. He has been a central figure in the resurgence of evangelicalism in the Church of England since the Second World War. He was Director, and then President, of the London Institute for Contemporary Christianity, and is now President of the Langham Partnership International. He has written many books and for over 30 years was a chaplain to the Queen. In 2006 he was made a CBE for services to Christian scholarship and the Christian world. His favourite relaxation is birdwatching.*

I believe in the Church of England. At least, I do and I don't. I do not believe in the Church of England, of course, in the sense that I believe in God – Father, Son and Holy Spirit – as the object of my confidence and worship. Yet I do believe in the Church of England in the sense that I am deeply grateful to be a member and a minister of it, and to be able to remain such with a good conscience. So I will start by sketching four distinctive features of the Church of England, which also constitute four reasons why I belong to it.

First, the Church of England is an *historical church*. It is, in fact, the church of the English people. It traces its origins back, not to Henry VIII and his matrimonial problems (the notorious 'King's matter'), but to the first century AD when the Roman legions were colonizing the empire, and merchants followed them, and among these soldiers and tradesmen there must have been followers of Jesus Christ. Both Tertullian and Origen round about the year AD 200 spoke of a church in England. St Alban died as a martyr for Christ, probably during the Decian persecution of AD 250. At the Synod of Arles in AD 314 there were three British bishops. So the Church of England is the historic church of this country.

Now this historical dimension is important today in a world that is busy cutting adrift from its historical roots. For the living God of the Bible is the God of history, the God of Abraham, Isaac and Jacob, the God of Moses and the prophets, the God of our Lord Jesus Christ and his apostles, and the God of the post-Apostolic Church. One of the weaknesses of the house-church movement is that it has little sense of history, little sense of continuity with the past.

Secondly, the Church of England is a *confessional church*. We move now from history to theology. According to 1 Timothy 3.15, the Church is 'the pillar *(stulos)* and bulwark *(hedraioma)* of the truth'. *Hedraioma* may mean either 'bulwark' or 'foundation'. In either case it holds a building firm, while pillars thrust the building aloft. So the Church is called to serve the truth, both holding it firm and holding it high for people to see. The Church of England, therefore, has doctrinal standards and a confession of faith. The Book of Common Prayer and the Thirty-Nine Articles remain the doctrinal basis of the Church of England, in spite of the weakening of the formula of assent and the arrival of the more recent service-books. Moreover, these standards affirm the supremacy of Scripture for salvation and the justification of sinners by grace alone, in Christ alone, through faith alone. These three doctrines are particularly dear to

8

evangelical believers, and they are plainly affirmed in our Anglican Articles.

It is true that there are a few church leaders who deny some fundamentals of the faith, and this is both a tragedy and a scandal. But the Church of England has never abandoned its confession of faith. It is a confessional church.

Thirdly, the Church of England is a *national church*. It is not a 'state' church like the continental Lutheran churches, but it is an 'established' church (recognized by law and given certain privileges), and – more importantly – it is a 'national' church because it has a national mission. In ideal and purpose, then, the Church of England is neither a sect nor a denomination, but the church of the nation, with a responsibility to be the nation's conscience, to serve the nation and to bring Christ to the nation.

It is perfectly true that in practice this ideal often breaks down, and that in our own day adjustments are needed. Nevertheless, although adaptations are necessary, the Church of England remains a national church.

Fourthly, the Church of England is a *liturgical church*. It has a Book of Common Prayer and a Common Worship service-book, containing services for public worship. Some say that set services inhibit spontaneity and the freedom of the Spirit. This does not have to be the case. Form and freedom are not necessarily incompatible with one another. Certainly, we welcome the greater flexibility which the new service-books have given us. But rightly they have not abandoned a liturgical framework and form.

Why should we value a liturgy? First, there is plenty of biblical warrant for liturgical forms. The New Testament contains many snatches of ancient hymns and credal statements, for Christians took this over from the Old Testament. Secondly, a liturgy enshrines truth and safeguards uniformity of doctrine. Thirdly, it gives a sense of solidarity both with the past and with the rest of the Church in the present. Fourthly, it protects the congregation from the worst idiosyncrasies of the clergy. Lastly, it is an aid to concentration and to congregational participation. These are great gains. They make me thankful that the Church of England is a liturgical church.

Here, then, are four reasons why I believe in the Church of England. It is the historical church of the English. It has a sound biblical, theological basis. It is entrusted with a national mission. And it has in its liturgy a worthy vehicle for the praise of Almighty God through Jesus Christ in the power of the Holy Spirit.

Having made these positive statements, however, many evangelicals feel uncomfortable in the Church of England today. The Church of England which I have described is more of an ideal than a reality. Some would dismiss it as a 'paper' church, and not one of flesh and blood, bones and sinews. At the same time, the evangelical movement has been growing in size, stature, maturity, scholarship and cohesion. It contains different strands (for example, reformed and charismatic), and is as much a coalition as a party. Simultaneously, there has been an assault on traditional Christian doctrine and morality. In consequence, the loyalty of ordinary church people has been strained. So what should we do?

The first option is *separation* or *secession* from the Church of England. To stay in a doctrinally mixed church, some would argue, is an intolerable compromise. It gives the impression that we condone heresy. So, in order to maintain our evangelical testimony without compromise, we should get out.

That is the position of independent evangelicals. Their overriding concern is to preserve the doctrinal purity of the

Church, which indeed is a right and proper concern. We should share their zeal for the truth, and their courage. But they tend to pursue the purity of the Church at the expense of its unity, for which they seem to have no comparable concern. To be sure, there could be an extreme situation (if the Church were officially to repudiate the Incarnation, for example) when the only possible course would be to secede, since then the Church would have ceased to be the Church. We need to remember, however, that the sixteenth-century Reformers were themselves very reluctant schismatics. They did not want to leave the Catholic Church. On the contrary, they dreamed of a reformed Catholicism, a Catholic Church reformed according to Scripture, and were concerned both for its purity and its unity. Calvin wrote to Cranmer in 1552, for example, that the separation of churches was 'among the greatest misfortunes of our century'. The 'bleeding' state of the body of Christ affected him so deeply, he added, that he would 'not hesitate to cross ten seas' if he could help. 'Indeed, if learned men were to seek a solid and carefully devised agreement according to the rule of Scripture ... I think that for my part I ought not to spare any trouble or dangers.' That is (or should be) exactly the position of Anglican evangelicals today.

The second option that is before us is the opposite extreme. It is that of *compromise*, and even *conformity*. This is the decision of some who say not only that they intend to stay in the Church of England at all costs, but that they would be willing to lose their distinctive evangelical witness.

I respect their desire to be responsible members of the Church of England, and (when it can be done with integrity) to minimize the differences between the traditions in the Church of England. But I think that their position is short-sighted. For we should have the courage, with humility, to bear witness to evangelical truth as we have been given to understand it. We claim no infallibility, and may be mistaken on certain points. We are open to have our minds changed if Scripture can be shown to require it. But we cannot conceal or smother our convictions. Our concern as evangelicals should certainly not be loyalty to a 'party'. Talk of a 'party' is a political concept. It conjures up toeing the party-line, submitting to the party whip and accepting the party discipline. Evangelical loyalty is not to a party, however, but to revealed truth, and in particular to the unique glory and adequacy of Jesus Christ.

The essence of the evangelical faith is that in Jesus Christ incarnate, crucified and exalted, God has spoken and acted decisively and finally for the salvation of the world. In consequence, Jesus Christ is God's last word to the world, and it is inconceivable that there should be any higher revelation than what he has given in his Son. Jesus Christ is also God's last deed for the salvation of the world, and it is inconceivable that anything should need to be added to it. Nothing can be added either to what God has spoken in Christ or to what God has done in Christ. Both were *hapax*, 'once and for all'. In Christ God's revelation and redemption are finished and complete.

That is why the hallmark of evangelicalism is an insistence on *sola scriptura* and *sola gratia*. They arise from *solus Christus*: Christ alone for revelation and redemption. Our concern, then, in maintaining a distinctive identity is not to be awkward or uncooperative or cussed or partisan. It is to be faithful to the unique glory of the person and work of our Lord Jesus Christ. It is, we believe, for the good of the Church and for the glory of God in Christ, that we should maintain our distinctive evangelical witness.

The third option is *comprehensiveness without compromise*, that is, staying in without caving in. Frankly, it is the most painful of the three options. The other two options are easier

12

because they are ways of cutting the Gordian knot. The first is to separate from everybody you disagree with, and so enjoy fellowship only with like-minded Christians. The second is to decline to maintain a distinctive testimony, and so regard all viewpoints as equally legitimate. These are opposite options (separation and compromise). But they have this in common: they are both ways of easing tension and escaping conflict. You either get out or you give in. The harder way, which involves walking a tightrope, is to stay in, while at the same time refusing to give in. This means living in a permanent state of tension, declining either to compromise or to secede.

Let me sum up. The way of separation is to pursue truth at the expense of unity. The way of compromise is to pursue unity at the expense of truth. The way of comprehension is to pursue truth and unity simultaneously, that is, to pursue the kind of unity commended by Christ and his apostles, namely unity in truth. Thus, Jesus prayed in John 17 for the truth, holiness, mission and unity of the Church, while in Ephesians 4 Paul affirmed that there is 'one Lord, one faith, one baptism'. Unity and truth always walk hand-in-hand in the New Testament.

I have described the third option as 'comprehension'. I now have to qualify this. For what is often called the 'comprehensiveness' of the Church of England can be sought in one or other of two ways. On the one hand, there is an unlimited and unprincipled kind of comprehensiveness, from which no one is excluded. On the other hand, there is a limited and principled kind of comprehensiveness which lays down clear lines of demarcation.

The unlimited and unprincipled kind is a doctrinal free-for-all, in which no opinion is prohibited, let alone condemned as heretical. Rather, every viewpoint is welcomed as a contribution to, and even ingredient of, the resulting pot-pourri. It is this that Bishop J.C. Ryle dubbed 'a kind of Noah's ark', roomy enough to accommodate both the clean and the unclean.

The best lampoon of this view was developed by Ronald Knox in the marvellous piece which he entitled 'Reunion all Round' and included in his *Essays in Satire*.[1] It was subtitled 'A plea for the inclusion within the Church of England of all Mohometans, Jews, Buddhists, Brahmins, Papists and Atheists'. In the new and universal Church which he saw emerging, 'nobody will be expected to recite the whole Creed', he wrote, 'but only such clauses as he finds relish in; it being anticipated that, with good fortune, a large congregation will usually manage in this way to recite the whole Formula between them'.

Having dealt with differences between Christians, and differences between theists, he came finally to 'the Problem of Reunion with the Atheists'. In their case: 'We have only one single Quarrel to patch up, namely, as to whether God exists or not.' So he proposed to the theologians that, as we believe God to be both immanent and yet transcendent, we should be able to reconcile ourselves to 'the last final Antinomy, that God is both Existent and Non-existent'. He ended: 'Thank God, in these days of Enlightenment and Establishment, everyone has a right to his own Opinions, and chiefly to the Opinion, That nobody else has a right to theirs ...'

This is not true ecumenism, however, but syncretism. Jesus our Lord and his apostles warned the Church of false teachers. And I am glad that the Church of England has always officially recognized that unity must be in truth and that comprehensiveness must be principled, for this is the historic understanding of what true Anglican comprehensiveness is all about. The purpose of the Elizabethan settlement in the sixteenth century was to unite the nation within a national church committed to the supremacy of Scripture and to the catholic creeds. As Dr Alec Vidler wrote:

> ... the conception of Anglican comprehensiveness has been taken to mean that it is the glory of the Church of England to hold together in juxtaposition as many varieties of Christian faith and practice as are willing to agree to differ, so that the Church is regarded as a sort of league of religions ... The principle of comprehension is that a church ought to hold the fundamentals of the faith, and at the same time allow for differences of opinion and of interpretation in secondary matters, especially rites and ceremonies ...[2]

It is a distinction which goes right back to the apostle Paul's insistence on loyalty to the Apostolic faith, alongside liberty of conscience on secondary issues.

So I do believe in the Church of England, in the rightness of belonging to it and of maintaining a faithful evangelical witness within it and to it. For I believe in the power of God's word and Spirit to reform and renew the Church. I also believe in the patience of God. Max Warren wrote that 'the history of the Church is the story of the patience of God'.[3] He was right. I do not think we have any liberty to be less patient than God has been.

NOTES

1. Ronald Knox, *Essays in Satire* (London: Sheed & Ward, 1928).
2. Alec Vidler, *Essays in Liberality* (London: SCM Press, 1957).
3. Max Warren, *I Believe in the Great Commission* (Sevenoaks: Hodder & Stoughton, 1979).

2

As it Was in the Beginning

P.D. James is an award-winning crime writer and President of the Society of Authors. Most of her detective novels have been filmed for television. She is a sometime Governor of the BBC and member of the Arts Council and of the British Council. She lists 'exploring churches' as one of her recreations, and is a Lay Patron of the Prayer Book Society. She was awarded the OBE in 1983 and created a Life Peer (as Baroness James of Holland Park) in 1991.

My love of the Church of England, and my continuing loyalty to it, has its roots in childhood, in family tradition and in nostalgia. No member of my family has been a priest (although my granddaughter is now married to one), but I was in a sense born in the odour of Anglicanism. My mother's father was headmaster of the choir school at Winchester Cathedral, and she was born in a house in the precincts. My paternal grandfather was organist at the garrison church in Portsmouth and wrote a number of anthems (none of which, as far as I know, is in use today). I was born in Oxford and, as both of my parents loved attending services in the college chapels, I was taken there in infancy, either in my mother's arms or left in my pram in the porch. (In those days, apparently, this was a safe expedient.) I like to think that from my earliest months,

16

liturgical music and Cranmer's marvellous cadences seeped
into my mind.

When we moved from Oxford to Ludlow on the Welsh
borders, I would be taken with my brother and sister every
Sunday to Evensong, one of the most satisfying services of
the Church spiritually and aesthetically, and still, I think,
my favourite. We attended a small church near Ludford
Bridge by the Teme where, in winter, there was a coke-
burning stove which would flare dramatically when the
wind changed, reminding me of the tongues of flame at
Whitsun. I can still picture my younger brother, curled
asleep against my mother; still recall the rather plump lady
who sat in the pew in front of ours and who had a huge
hatpin which seemed, to my childish eyes, to pierce right
through the back of her head.

In the pew in which we invariably sat there was a
leather-bound Prayer Book with a brass clasp. It was
always there and became for me an object of intense desire,
which I had to resist the temptation to take home with me.
It was my first intimation of the physicality of the book as
something beautiful as well as desirable, and my earliest
experience of the pleasure and excitement of handling its
smooth, rich-smelling cover and turning the pages. I first
steeped myself in the history and the romance of the Prayer
Book when I was about ten years old and would read it to
alleviate the *longueurs* of the sermon, which in those days
sometimes lasted for 40 minutes. I remember how
fascinated I was by the note at the end of the service for
the Communion of the Sick:

> In this time of plague, sweat, or such other like
> contagious times of sickness and disease, when none of
> the Parish or neighbours can be gotten to commu-
> nicate with the sick in their houses for fear of the

infection, upon special request of the diseased, the Minister may only communicate with him.

To someone who was already dimly aware that she would one day become a novelist, these words presented to my imagination a vivid picture of priestly heroism and self-sacrifice: the deserted village, the plague-stricken victim, the lonely priest making his communion in the sickroom, breathing in the fatal contamination.

Later I went to a church school in Ludlow, where the parish priest would visit each week to teach us the Collect and instruct us in its meaning. So those marvellous prayers, at once so beautifully constructed, so simple and yet so pregnant with meaning, entered early into my consciousness to become part of my religious and literary heritage and to help make me a writer. When we moved house we worshipped at the great parish church of St Leonard, where my father sang in the choir and on occasion carried the processional cross, a privilege which aroused in me mixed emotions – family pride and a terror that he might drop it.

The Church of England in my childhood was the national Church in a very special sense: the visible symbol of the nation's moral and religious aspirations in a country which – despite great differences of class, wealth and privilege – was unified by generally accepted values and by a common tradition, history and culture, just as the Church was unified by Cranmer's magnificent liturgy. There were, of course, varieties of practice, and little superficial resemblance between the multi-candled ceremonial, the incense and Stations of the Cross found in the extreme High Church, and the simplicities of an evangelical church which could have been mistaken for a nonconformist chapel. But it was possible to attend different churches – on holiday, for example – and feel immediately at home, finding in the pew not a service sheet with a series number but the familiar and unifying Book of Common Prayer.

Today I frequently hear people and families referred to as being Christian as if they were members of a minority and slightly eccentric sect. In my childhood the majority of the population, whether or not they regularly attended a place of worship, thought of themselves as Christians, and most described themselves as C of E. The English have always respected and felt a devotion to their Church, provided they are not expected regularly to attend its services. The importance of the Church of England as the national Church was perhaps most clearly shown on Armistice Day, when whole communities gathered in their parish church, united in sorrowful remembrance. To be born in 1920, two years after the end of the slaughter of a generation, was to be aware from one's earliest years of a universal grieving which was almost part of the air one breathed.

It would be simplistic to give the impression that all was well with the Church of my childhood, although to describe it in the familiar phrase, 'the Conservative Party at prayer', would be misleading. But the Church, like most institutions, reflects the cultural and class divisions of the age. Although it was becoming increasingly uncommon for the more privileged worshippers to have their own pews, there was still a difference in the make-up of congregations at the Sunday services. Families like ours who couldn't afford to employ servants were more commonly seen at Evensong than at Matins. And the Church of England was male-dominated. Women had not begun to assert their right to more prominent participation in the worship and priests tended to come from one section of society.

My earliest experience of communal singing was in church, and hymns are one of the Anglican Church's greatest gifts to the English-speaking world. To judge from the Sunday evening television programme *Songs of Praise*, they remain popular with hundreds and thousands who are not necessarily regular attenders at services. They seem, indeed, to be in some sense part of our national folk-memory. Some are great poetry, others are Victorian rewriting of the originals, and some are undoubtedly banal or sentimental, but nearly all the most familiar and the best retain their power. In the best, words and music are indissolubly wedded, and both remain so strongly embedded in my consciousness that, even when not in church, I can find myself singing the old favourites. My mother particularly loved the triumphant 'For All the Saints', and in childhood I certainly preferred the more vigorous and celebratory hymns, particularly at Easter when the church was filled with spring flowers, and the choir – their surplices newly starched and dazzling white – processed down the aisle in a wave of triumphant organ music and Easter song. The evening hymns 'The Day Thou Gavest, Lord, is Ended' and 'Abide with Me' still have an extraordinary power to move me, bringing to memory those childhood services of Evensong, the candlelit faces of the choir, the gathering darkness outside and a feeling of universal sadness, which as a child I could experience but not comprehend.

The Church of England has, of course, a magnificent architectural heritage. All my life I have received delight, and indeed spiritual sustenance, not only from visits to the large cathedrals, but to village churches. Some – particularly in East Anglia, which I love – are as large and magnificent as cathedrals; others small, sometimes difficult to find, but always holding for me a numinous peace born of centuries of prayer. It is a sadness to me that most of our cathedrals now charge for admission. I can understand that they desperately need the money and it does seem unfair that tourists who are not coming to worship and who are paying the tour operators should not contribute to the upkeep of these great national monuments. But I still find it disconcerting to confront commercialism, even while I recognize the necessity of the cause.

As Anglicans, we should also recognize that the majority of our cathedrals and country churches, now so redolent of the beliefs and practices of what is still the national Church, are inherited from Roman Catholicism. In a very real sense they belong not to one denomination but to Christendom and, indeed, to all who find within these walls something of the beauty of holiness and a temporary refuge from the getting and spending of our frantic world. But all – whether evangelical, high Anglican, or somewhere in between; the village churches and the quiet corners of great cathedrals – seem to me essentially Anglican in their silent uncluttered peace, and I never enter them without feeling that I have come home.

Unhappily, the Church of England is today riven by more dissensions than I can remember in my lifetime, and one result has been a falling away from the tolerance for which the Church has always been respected. The divisions have, of course, been rooted by fundamental doctrinal differences, about what the Church actually is, the primacy of Scripture and the nature of the Eucharist; compromise is hardly possible, since opinions on both sides are held with passionate conviction as a matter of conscience. Similarly, on matters of order: those who sincerely believe, for example, that homosexuality is a sin, rather than an inborn sexual orientation which is as ineradicable and valid as heterosexuality, and claim to find their authority in

Scripture, are unlikely ever to accept the ordination of practising homosexuals, any more than those who take the view that the priest represents Christ at the altar during the Holy Communion can accept a woman in this role. If these opposing views are to be accommodated within one Church, there has to be charity – indeed Christian love – between opposing factions; unhappily, in some parishes and dioceses this loving kindness has been notably absent.

Much that has happened in recent years, including the neglect of the Book of Common Prayer, is saddening for those of us born into the Anglican Church, but it does not destroy our love for Anglicanism or our continued need to pursue our path towards the understanding of God within this familiar fold. And I remember – as surely do others – the faithfulness and courage shown by many hundreds of priests, particularly in inner-city parishes, who are trying to witness to Christ in a largely unbelieving materialistic age and to bring the faith to people deeply distressed by deprivation. It would, of course, be both inaccurate and presumptuous to claim that Anglicanism has a unique history of piety. Other Christian denominations have their saints and heroes, and their ministers too have served their people with love, devotion and courage. This is particularly impressive today when priests are often at serious risk of physical assault and, in the most deprived areas, share a great number of the problems and hardships of poverty.

What I have valued all my life in the national Church has been respect for learning, tolerance and inclusiveness. Like Elizabeth I, the Church of England does not 'make windows into men's souls'. For many people, religion is less a matter of absolute certainty than a lifelong searching for God, and many thousands over the centuries have undertaken this pilgrimage within the Church of England, believing what they can believe and taking comfort from the order and dignity of the services, the incomparable beauty of the liturgy and the all-embracing charity.

The Reverend Sydney Smith, that notable nineteenth-century divine, when advising a lady on how to overcome depression, advised – among such practical matters as keeping her sitting-room cheerful and stoking up good fires – that she should be regular in the practice of rational religion. For him, one of the major virtues of the Church of England was its rationality – a virtue not often associated with religious faith. This rationality, combined with common sense, is illustrated by the words in the preface to the Book of Common Prayer:

> It hath been the wisdom of the Church of England, ever since the first compiling of her Publick Liturgy, to keep the mean between the two extremes, of too much stiffness in refusing, and of too much easiness in admitting any variation from it. For, as on the one side common experience sheweth, that where a change hath been made of things advisedly established (no evident necessity so requiring) sundry inconveniences have thereupon ensued; and those many times more and greater than the evils that were intended to be remedied by such change.

It is a pity that our legislators so seldom take this advice.

The same practical note is set in the preface on the Ceremonies of the Church.

> The minds of men are so diverse that some think it a great matter of conscience to depart from a piece of the least of their Ceremonies, they be so addicted to their old custom. And again on the other side, some be so

new-fangled, that they would innovate all things, and so despise the old, that nothing can like them, but that is new.

This love of the middle way, of accommodation to different views of an all-embracing tolerance, has been an essential part of Anglican thinking and practice.

I rejoice too in the rich heritage of Anglican writing, both devotional and secular, particularly the poets whose faith has influenced their work; among the names that come to mind are John Donne, Thomas Traherne, William Cowper, T.S. Eliot, R.S. Thomas and John Betjeman. I have recently been reading *Love's Redeeming Work*,[1] an anthology of writing within the Anglican tradition, which draws together the works of major writers who have helped to form the theology and spirituality of the contemporary Church, from the sixteenth century to the present day. Among them is part of a sermon by John Jebb, who was born in 1775 and who in 1822 became Bishop of Limerick. It sums up wonderfully what I value in our national Church:

> The Church of England steers a middle course. She reveres the Scripture: she respects tradition. She encourages investigation: but she checks presumption. She bows to the authority of ages: but she owns no living master upon earth. She rejects alike the wild extravagance of unauthorised opinion, and the tame subjection of compulsory belief. Where the Scripture clearly and freely speaks, she receives its dictates as the voice of God. When the Scripture is either not clear, or explicit; or when it may demand expansion and illustration, she refers her sons to an authoritative standard of interpretation; but a standard, which it is their privilege to apply for themselves.

Even when my religious life has been at a low ebb and my churchgoing erratic, I have never contemplated leaving the Church of England. The tie is a bloodline and to break it would be as meaningless and unthinkable as rejecting my family. As I grow older, I find that I believe less of the dogma of Christianity but hold more firmly to those things which I do believe. I would find no greater certainty in any other Christian Church, and perhaps few of us in this world can expect certainty. Within Anglicanism I undertake my earthly pilgrimage. I hope, I trust, and I believe what I can believe. The Church of England is the one into which I was baptized, whose liturgy helped to make me a writer, whose sacraments have comforted and sustained me through a long life lived in tumultuous times, and it is this Church – Catholic and Reformed, tolerant, inclusive, flawed but beautiful, and peculiarly English – in which I shall die.

NOTE

1. *Love's Redeeming Work*, comp. Geoffrey Rowell, Kenneth Stevenson and Rowan Williams (Oxford: Oxford Univesity Press, 2001).

3

Living a Life

Anne Atkins *is author of three novels:* The Lost Child, On our Own *and* A Fine and Private Place. *Her latest book,* Agony Atkins, *is a compilation of her robustly Christian and often hilarious agony aunt column which ran for several years in the* Daily Telegraph; *before that she wrote* Child Rearing for Fun, *a book to give parents confidence and make them laugh out loud. One of her many doctrinally orthodox 'Thought for the Day' on Radio 4's* Today *programme reputedly had the distinction of prompting the first ever complaint to the BBC from the usually rather sleepy Church of England Press Office. Anne lives in the south of England with her clergyman husband, their five children and rather more large animals than is strictly necessary for a quiet life.*

'I see myself primarily as a Christian, rather than an Anglican or an evangelical, or any other label. What matters is that Jesus saved me, not that I adhere to any particular clique in the club. (If you prefer, the important thing is being a Christian, not what type of Christian you are.) This is the message of the New Testament: that all believers are part of one holy, catholic and apostolic Church; we are all equally members of the same family.

But I admit that if someone were to ask me, "What kind of a Christian are you?" I would say (after the obvious answer, "a very bad one") that I am an Anglican: I am a member of the Church of England.

There are three reasons for my allegiance. The first is intellectual: I regard the Anglican Church as the most theologically faithful church, and the Book of Common Prayer, the Thirty-Nine Articles and the creeds as accurate interpretations of Scripture. The next reason is pragmatic: I believe the parish system to be very effective, the Church being a national Church that belongs to everyone in the parish, and therefore the country. You might not set out to invent it that way but, having inherited it, I believe it is a wonderfully effective way of sharing and living the gospel. Finally, I confess, my attachment to the Church of England is accidental and familial: I am Anglican by birth, brought up in a Christian home within the Church of England.

This last means that being an Anglican, for me, is also bound up with all sorts of things that are not solely rational or logical. It's my home: it matters to me in the same way that love of my home city matters to me, or the love of my family – they are not necessarily better than anyone else's, but they belong to me. So I love the Church of England because it's mine, rather than because it's necessarily better than any other Church: a personal loyalty, as well as an intellectual choice. It's a happenstance of birth that I find myself within it, and part of my attachment is sentimental and emotional, in the same way that you hang on to your great-grandfather's high-chair.

Christianity was in the air we breathed as children. My parents didn't talk about their faith all the time, but I saw them living out a Christian life every day, and in every way. My father has become much more outspoken about his beliefs now that he's living in a more secular, counter-Christian culture; when I was younger, I saw his personal conviction in action, rather than in anything he necessarily said. I've often thought that in years to come, when I look back on his life, I'll remember him on his knees in King's College Chapel, Cambridge: that image of him, face hidden, silently leaning on his arms on his cushioned reading-desk, in prayer, seems symbolic of his life. He was headmaster of the King's Choir School in Cambridge, so that's where I grew up; and the soaring chapel, radiant with that ethereal, almost eternal, music provided me with my spiritual home.

Naturally, my parents were the primary influence on my life; thanks to them my heart was rooted in Christianity. But it was my older brother who helped me to an intellectual commitment. He introduced me to evangelicalism: to the concept of Scripture being reliable and the idea that faith should be approached rationally and with some sort of intellectual rigour. After school in Cambridge I went to university in Oxford, where I found among most of the believing, practising Christians a commitment to Scripture that I hadn't been aware of as I grew up; so it was there that I became intellectually as well as emotionally committed to Christianity.

At Oxford I met Shaun, who was President of the OICCU (the university Christian Union – by far the biggest university society) and already destined for ministry. We were married after Finals, and moved to Cambridge where he started training at Ridley Hall. For the first time, I found myself surrounded by undiluted evangelicalism. That was quite alien to me, particularly the attitude to women which was unlike anything I had grown up with. It seemed to me that the culture of a couple of generations earlier had been mistaken for the teachings of Christianity, and it was this that prompted me to write my first book.[1] I thought, if this is genuine Christianity then I've got some radical rethinking to do; but if it isn't then I want to reject it robustly. So I embarked on three years (or rather three pregnancies) of studying the Scriptures to see whether Christianity really teaches that women are preordained to make flapjacks and starch surplices while men save the world, or whether this had just been assumed by a bunch of rather self-important and over-earnest ordinands and their wonderfully unselfish but slightly mousey wives. Happily, and to my immense relief, I concluded that it was the latter.

If I had found such injunctions in Scripture I wouldn't have rejected Christianity. I just would have been miserable. Because I believe Scripture to be paramount, I would have had to submit myself to it and adjust my own ideas of what was appropriate for men and women. In fact, I discovered St Paul to be a rousing and radical feminist: teaching that a man doesn't have authority over his own body but his wife does, for instance; and that husbands must lay down their lives for their wives; and women must be educated and should feel free to stay single; and married couples should enjoy frequent love-making. There is an exhilarating equality throughout Scripture, supremely in Jesus's life, but also specifically applied by St Paul.

Apart from the Bible itself, I take the central tenets of Anglicanism to be the Apostles' Creed, the Book of Common Prayer and the Thirty-Nine Articles, all of which I heartily embrace. I'm cautious about the so-called "Three Pillars" of Christian truth – Scripture, reason and tradition – because I think they're too easily used as a way of justifying one's own subjective argument. How do you weigh them up? If Scripture seems to say something that is unreasonable, or tradition to have gone against what is scriptural, how do you choose what is authoritative? So I would put them in order. I want to value Scripture first, because it's there that God speaks. Then reason, because I'm an Anglican rather than a Roman Catholic, and also quite a fan of mankind. Lastly, I am influenced by tradition in my interpretation of Scripture, because the Church is usually facing in approximately the right direction. If Christians have traditionally understood a certain passage in a particular way, it's true that they could always have been wrong (and I believe some passages have long been misinterpreted), but it's more likely that I'll get it wrong myself. The Church, however flawed she is, has understood the essential doctrines of the faith more or less accurately for most of history.

So if we take something like, say, the ordination of women (now a bit passé, I'm afraid) the first question I want to ask is, what does Scripture say? Taking all the relevant texts in their various contexts into account, I believe Scripture allows women's ministry on a par with men's, but doesn't insist on it. It's permissible, but not compulsory. This being satisfactorily established, we are now free to ask the next question, what does reason tell us? Personally, I think it would have been absolutely loopy for God to have given women the same gifts as men, then said we are not to use them; this does not seem reasonable at all. So reason reinforces my interpretation of Scripture, that women's ordination is allowable. Lastly, what about tradition? For much of Christianity's history, I believe we have been unnecessarily restricting ourselves to men's ministry (since God's word does not forbid a woman's authoritative role); on the other hand, we have not been disobedient (because his word doesn't specifically command it). Scripture allows it; reason commends it; tradition has done without it. Conclusion: women's ministry is acceptable, but not essential.

Now, let's take a currently more contentious issue. What about certain sexual relationships? There seems to me no escaping the fact that Scripture forbids sexual intimacy outside marriage. So this topic doesn't get beyond first base:

however unreasonable it seems, we must submit ourselves to the doctrine that marriage is the only context for sex. Scripture is unequivocal on it, and Scripture is the best guidance God has given us. There is no place for reason to protest or tradition to argue, because Scripture has left no loophole.

One thing I hugely admire about the Roman Catholic Church, which I sometimes wish we had, is its unapologetic certainty, its preparedness to be an unpopular and unfashionable minority. It knows that its strength lies in proclaiming its beliefs and doctrines, even when the world is shouting in protest that such outmoded ideas are outrageous. I think we, as the Church of England, lack the confidence to be outspoken, which is a weakness and a shame.

But we have compensating qualities: a personal relationship with God, and an individual responsibility for the intellectual content of our faith. Was the Reformation a Good Thing? Of course it was. Leaving aside the devastating theft and ravishment of the cultural wealth of the monasteries – an absolute outrage – the English Reformation was spiritually one of the proudest moments of our history. Something I love about Protestantism in general and Anglicanism in particular is hearing the preacher, standing six foot above contradiction, telling me to open my Bible so that I can check he gets it right and correct him if necessary. Thanks to the Reformation, the sermon is a dialogue not a lecture.

Anglicanism is supremely inclusive. The parochial system is a very effective way of living as salt within the community. The Church belongs to everyone in the country, regardless of his or her profession of faith. We all have a right to be baptized in the Church of England; we all have a right to get married in the Church of England; we all have a right to be on an electoral roll. Sometimes over-zealous clergy say that their baptism policy is not to include children of non-believers, but an Anglican cleric has no right to do this: he cannot decide on someone else's spiritual status. You can be a Hindu and still be on the electoral roll and have a right to vote at the AGM, and surely this is what the Gospel is about: Jesus died for everyone, of every nation and race, every creed and background.

Synod's decision to allow some but not all divorcees to be remarried in church was a pernicious undermining of that superbly egalitarian principle: for the first time, the parish priest has had to stand in judgement over his parishioners and say that one couple can get married in church but another can't – and he is the one who decides. For the priest to be called to discriminate over the laity like this is profoundly unAnglican, and I believe wrong.

Anglicanism is by nature non-judgemental. The whole community has a stake in it. We are all entitled to be members of our parish church. Of course this inclusiveness has a negative side: the sort of clichéd, bumbling, politically correct episcopate where no bishop dares say anything decisive in case John Humphrys interviews him unsympathetically the next morning. But the positive side is that we're all in it together. I want to be in a church where my liberal brothers and sisters and my Anglo-Catholic brothers and sisters and my evangelical brothers and sisters can all worship side by side, because I believe we have far more in common than our differences.

When Shaun was ordained, we moved first of all to Barnet in North London. He was fortunate in having as his first vicar someone who was very Anglican and did Anglicanism very well: it was Anglicanism at its best.

I embarked on Shaun's ministry (if that's not too paradoxical a phrase) with no expectations of myself at all, other than of being an ordinary member of the congregation; I didn't see myself as having any other role. An older vicar's wife asked me, "Are you expected to do much visiting?", and I realized that I hadn't the faintest idea: it had never occurred to me to be at all interested in what the expectations of me were. In Shaun's first week, Michael (his vicar) said to him, "You must tell Anne that surplices are very difficult to iron." When he came home and told me this, I said, "Why on earth would I want to know that?" I was genuinely completely mystified. (Shaun once said, rather forlornly, that when we lived in suburbia he was the only man in the street who didn't have his shirts ironed for him.)

There, and in our subsequent parishes, I came from the principle of being an ordinary, committed member of the congregation. What this meant when we later went to a fairly moribund church was that we all got really stuck in because there was so much that needed doing. The children and I became very involved. They prayed a Sunday school into existence; I started an instrumental ensemble and then a choir. But I saw this as simply being part of our Christian life, not necessarily because we were a clergy family.

Since then my views have changed somewhat, and been enriched by experience: there's no specific role a clergy family has, but I do believe we're called upon to model the Christian life even more than other Christians. Of course we should all do this; but lay families can afford more mistakes. St Paul again is clear on this. It doesn't mean that some are better Christians than others, but if certain things have happened in your life you may serve the Gospel better from within the laity rather than the clergy. For instance, I believe it's a mistake that we now have divorced and remarried clergy. This is not because they're not such good Christians as those who are fortunate enough still to be in their first marriages – of course not – but the clergy are expected to live out the ideal of the Christian life in a way that the laity aren't necessarily able to.

This does mean there is a risk of putting clergy on a pedestal. I realized this for the first time when one of our children became ill: she has had a very long, very painful and debilitating mental illness. There's a huge taboo about mental illness; even among a congregation where we were very much loved and part of a close-knit family, there were still considerable misunderstandings. It was when friends and parishioners became frightened at seeing us struggle that I realized how disillusioning it was for them to see that we were people who could go through pain. But that's also a part of living the Gospel. What we experienced then was Anglicanism at its best – not just Anglicanism, but Christianity – and very precious: we were part of a family, we could explain what we were enduring, and people came to understand and share in our sorrow.

And of course being a father to a sick child is as much as part of Shaun's ministry as standing up in the pulpit or chairing the Parochial Church Council. A clergyman isn't on a salary: he is given a stipend. He's not doing a job: he's living a life within the community. When Pope John Paul II was dying, and so ill that there was talk about him stepping down to allow somebody else to run the show, Clifford Longley did a marvellous "Thought for the Day" explaining that Christian leadership is not about doing, or organizing, or running meetings – it's about being. Once upon a time, the vicar often wouldn't necessarily spend many hours doing what we think of as the job: he'd be collecting butterflies, or writing books, or educating his children. There is something rather fine about living a life, albeit rather an eccentric one, rather than performing in a job. "Career clergyman" is, to my mind, an oxymoron; if you want a career, why not join the Civil Service?

One of the endearing things about Anglicanism is that it does have daft, bumpy bits. But the other side of the coin is that the Church of England also tolerates enormous muddles, which can be infuriating. A typical one is that the Church of England has half-modernized itself, but only half. We've sold off almost all of the wonderful vicarages, for instance; of course we all know why, and there are legitimate economic arguments for this. But we don't do it properly: why don't we give all the church buildings to English Heritage and let them have the expense of running them; sell off all the vicarages altogether; pay a cleric a proper graduate salary and let him (or her) buy his own house and do a nine to five job with proper time off? (Not that I am advocating this, but there are arguments for it.) Doctors have done it: why not the clergy? But that would be far too businesslike for the Church of England. So instead we've abolished the one thing that gave the parson security (his freehold); we've done away with his rambling old house that enabled him and his family to have a rather untidy but astonishingly effective ministry; we've shoved him into an executive modern box which means he can be socially pigeonholed somewhere firmly in the middle class (but not too far up it); and we have the worst of all worlds. He has no job security, a laughable stipend, someone else's (usually very naff) choice of housing and nowhere to live when he retires (which he is now forced to do). Most of this mess is modern, and much of it thanks to General Synod – in itself a breathtaking waste of money.

The Book of Common Prayer was a great equalizer, globally as well as locally: once upon a time you could walk into an Anglican church anywhere in the world and feel at home in the service. Now, of course, it's divisive because so few people are familiar with it; so something that was intended as accessible has become upper-middle-class and sadly we have to keep retranslating the language. At heart, Anglicanism has traditionally been remarkably egalitarian: clergy and choir alike equalized by their robes; large vicarages known not to be symbols of personal wealth but working buildings; the lasting language of Cranmer deliberately grafted from Saxon and Latin roots for ploughman and peer alike. All these things have been mistakenly thought to be divisive, and largely been abolished.

One of the great strengths of Anglicanism is that it's local. Of course it's important that we are also part of a great big global family. But there is always a tendency to heresy in the heart of man, and what makes Anglicanism strong is that it's rooted in the parish, rooted in the place, so if a province like ECUSA (the Episcopal Church of the United States of America) errs and strays ... well, it's a shame but it doesn't bring down the rest of us. Similarly, individuals within the Church of England may go off the rails; bishops or archbishops may wander off the pathway; the General Synod may take a heretical decision ... but the rest of us are still here, in the Church of England, in our parishes.

I'm an Anglican because it's my home. My life could still go on if the Church of England no longer existed, in a way that it couldn't if Christianity ceased to be true – if that happened, I could no longer be. My Anglican allegiance is temporal; my Christian faith is a matter of life or death. So it is only a matter of this world that I'm an Anglican: my Anglicanism will pass away. But, as long as the Church of England is here, she and I are part of each other.'

NOTE

1. *Split Image: Male and Female after God's Likeness* (Sevenoaks: Hodder & Stoughton, 1987).

4

One Common Humanity

Emeka (Eleazar Chukwuemeka) Anyaoku, an *Ndichie Chief of Obosi in Nigeria, is chairman of the Presidential Advisory Council on Foreign Relations in Nigeria, International President of the World Wide Fund for Nature, President of the Royal Commonwealth Society and the Royal Africa Society, a trustee of the British Museum and Vice-Chairman of the Governing Board of the South Centre. He was Secretary-General of the Commonwealth from 1990–2000 and Nigeria's Foreign Minister in 1983.*

'When I was growing up, Anglicanism was representative of the colonial authority. My great-grandfather was one of those who, in 1882, thumbed the treaty ceding my part of eastern Nigeria (now "Abutchi" – Obosi – in Anambra State) to the protection of Queen Victoria. He could not convert, because of his standing in society, but was wise enough to have his eldest son educated by a Church Missionary Society (CMS) priest, the Reverend William Blackett (who was of Barbadian origin, but came out to Nigeria from England). So I was born into an Anglican family: I am a second-generation Anglican, because my father was the first convert.

My mother's father also could not convert, so he sent his daughter to live with the first ordained Anglican priest in

39

our community, the Reverend Abel Ekpunobi. He had been one of the first Anglican converts, and was baptized in 1882. My mother became a convert and went to an Anglican school. My parents had an arranged marriage. The fact that they were both converts from animism obviously played a part in that.

My father was baptized at the age of 14; when his father died, he became an almost fanatical Anglican. We used to worship ancestors, and the symbol of ancestral authority and spirituality was the "Ikenga" which was housed in a small shrine at the centre of the family compound. When, following the death of my grandfather, my father became head of the family, he had the Ikenga and the shrine removed to the home of his cousin, who was not a convert. At the time, he was thought to be a little crazy, but the shrine has remained in the home of that family ever since. When I inherited my father's responsibilities, I didn't see fit to bring it back.

I am the eldest of six children and we were all baptized as babies. My family stood out locally: apart from my father's immediate family (which included my uncle and my aunt), my father's cousins were still animists. Growing up, I took part in those traditional practices that my father judged not to be pagan. For instance, at the age of 12, I was inducted into local masquerade society. The widespread belief then was that masquerades were not human beings but spirits. When a boy comes of age, therefore, he is inducted into the society in a way which enables him to become a masquerade – to put on the attire of a masquerade and to assume the position of being a spirit.

Being Anglican was a source of pride, because it carried with it the badge of education. Going to school when those around you weren't going to school, you felt a little superior. But the wider family ties were strong enough to mean that we were never separated, even though we had chosen a different way of life. We still associated closely with our relatives, who didn't go to church or to school.

CMS had founded both churches and schools in eastern Nigeria. My father went to a CMS school, and I too went to a CMS primary school, and then on to a boarding-school which had itself been founded by a man who had studied at London and Oxford Universities and had grown up in the Anglican tradition. He had laid down very strong Anglican foundations for the school.

He was also very politically aware: he had been in England during the Second World War, and he taught us that your religion was different from your politics. I was confirmed at the age of 16. By then, I was able to differentiate between religion and colonialism, and also between the different denominations (Roman Catholicism was then doing very well locally). I had become comfortable with Anglicanism, and as a boy I was a very keen Scout. Scouting was not strictly religious, but in my part of the world it was bound up with the Anglican tradition. Although Scouting was also associated with the colonial regime, its attractions for young people outweighed the drawbacks.

My part of Nigeria progressed towards independence without any great struggle with colonialism. There were incidents, such as the Women's Riot (when they refused to pay tax) in 1929, and the shooting and killing of several coal-miners in Enugu: these were landmarks of the agitation to end colonialism. However, it was quite unlike eastern and southern Africa where there was a real struggle (the Mau-Mau in Kenya, and the liberation wars of southern Africa). It was therefore much easier in Nigeria to make a choice based on conviction, independent of the colonial associations.

When I left school, I taught for 18 months in another private school with an Anglican foundation, before going to

University College Ibadan to read Classics. I was then recruited into what was at the time the Colonial Development Corporation (it became the Commonwealth Development Corporation), and was sent to London to do various training courses. I worked at the CDC head office in Hill Street before being posted back to their regional office in Lagos.

My responsibilities included all CDC-supported projects in West Africa – not only Nigeria, but Ghana, Sierra Leone, the Gambia and southern Cameroon. When the Nigerian government was negotiating a loan from CDC to support its projects, the then-Chairman of CDC came out to Nigeria on a visit. We had a meeting with the Prime Minister, who asked a number of questions about CDC-supported projects in West Africa, so I did quite a bit of the talking. When we were leaving, the Prime Minister called me back and said, "Look – the British have many experts but we are just beginning. You must come and work for the Nigerian government. I'd like to see you in the Nigerian Diplomatic Service."

Four years after that move, in 1966, I was recruited to the new Commonwealth Secretariat and in 1989 I was appointed Commonwealth Secretary-General. During my years in the service of the Commonwealth Secretariat, I travelled very extensively; still today, as President of the Royal Commonwealth Society and of the Royal African Society, and as the International President of the World Wide Fund for Nature, I travel often to many Commonwealth and other countries also. In my travels, I worship at different churches around the world and I have never found worshipping in a church of which I am not a regular member a handicap: it seems natural to me that you should worship wherever you are.

I believe that my faith has made it possible for me to hold on to my career commitments, because essentially I am a believer in one common humanity: that, to me, is the core belief of the Commonwealth. It doesn't matter where you were born, or what is your background – obviously we are all differently conditioned by environment and opportunity; we have different skin colours and hold different religious beliefs – but we share a common humanity. My faith has underpinned my work in terms of the two greatest laws – to love God with all your heart and soul and mind and strength, and to love your neighbour as yourself. I understand the second of those as the theology of one common humanity, and it has been central to my work.

Both at home and in the course of my travels I have seen some very good things done in the name of Christianity, but some very bad ones also, notably the perversion of religion in apartheid South Africa (where there were some advocates of apartheid who sought to root their advocacy in their religious beliefs). Some of the things done in the name of religion have been shocking to me. On the other hand, in my own country, CMS established, for instance, Iyi Enu Hospital, where I was born and which at that time was the best hospital in that whole part of Nigeria.

An ongoing debate in Nigeria (which has now been settled in principle, though not in practice) was the return of mission schools to the missions. When they were religious schools, whether Anglican or Roman Catholic, they were disciplined institutions where children were well brought up, but in the early 1970s the military government (under General Gowon, who was Head of State and himself a committed Christian) decreed that mission schools should cease to exist and the State took them over. Standards deteriorated and discipline broke down, so years later there was a political debate which resolved that the schools should

43

be returned to the missions. The missions are able to take them back, but the biggest stumbling-block seems to be the teachers' unions, which have been resisting the change because teachers are better off (in their conditions of service) when the government is their employer.

When I was asked by Archbishop George Carey to be a part of the commission (under Douglas Hurd) looking at the role of the Archbishop of Canterbury, one of the statistics that interested me was that the Nigerian church was the fastest-growing in the Anglican Communion. Today there are new challenges arising from Anglicanism in the UK for the rest of the Anglican Communion. Some of these challenges pose a personal dilemma to people like me. One is the ordination of women, which I have fully accepted, and I am quite comfortable with the prospect of the appointment of women bishops. What I am not comfortable with is the movement for gay ordination: that is particularly unacceptable to African Christians, which is why it's such a problem for the African provinces of the Anglican Communion. What the Archbishop of Nigeria has been articulating has the support, not only of Nigeria but also of the rest of Africa (with the possible exception of South Africa because of the Western influence there). The evolution of liberal philosophy in countries of the North has produced things like the gay movement, but in Africa by and large the population is against it.

I wouldn't think in terms of leaving the Anglican Church, but I would think of changing my place of worship. I don't think I would want to receive communion from a self-confessed practising gay priest, nor would I want to belong to a diocese headed by a self-confessed practising gay bishop. This is an important issue for me, but it wouldn't drive me out of the Church. I have nothing at all against gay people, but I don't believe that self-confessed practising gay people should have a place in the leadership of the Church.

One of the great strengths of Anglicanism is that it does not impose too rigid a form of practice on the believer or practitioner. Clearly there is a Christian code of conduct, which any believer should aspire to live by, but religious regimentation does not exist in Anglicanism. On the other hand, this may inadvertently promote a level of idleness as non-attendance at church comes more easily to an Anglican than to a Roman Catholic. Going to worship at least once every seven days is something I think every Christian and certainly every Anglican should aspire to.

Essentially, my wife Bunmi and I have three churches. In London, we belong to St Michael's (Chester Square); we belong to the community of St John's in Lagos; and then of course we belong to my parents' church, St Andrew's in Obosi, where I was born. That's my family church, and that's where our ancestral home is.

When I am there, I fulfil my traditional role as *Ichie* ("Chief") Adazie Obosi. There are nine *Ichies*: they are the king-makers, the ones who determine, when a vacancy occurs, who the next king will be. Our kingship is not directly hereditary: there are four branches of one original royal family, and any first-born prince from these four families could become king.

In 1989, after my election as Secretary-General, I took some time to reflect and spent six months living in Obosi. The then British Assistant Under-Secretary of State, Sir Roger Tomkys, was paying an official visit to Nigeria and came to stay with us. He arrived on the eve of a reception my community was giving to honour my new appointment, so he came to the reception as a guest. The king addressed the

45

gathering in my mother-tongue, which is Ibo, and I translated for my British guests. After a while, in deference to our august visitors, the king said that he would speak in a language they could understand. So he began to speak in English and my visitor turned to me and asked wonderingly, "How can the king speak such good English?" I said, "He left Imperial College London with a first-class degree." That king's father came to London for Queen Victoria's Jubilee.

Being a chief means that at home in Obosi I cannot eat in public. I can be entertained in the house of the king or another chief like me, but if it was a public occasion there would have to be a private room where the chiefs could eat. When we entertain at home, we can eat in our dining-room, but I would not eat at an outdoor event.

Nor, at home, would I ever sit with my back to the door, in keeping with a tradition that had its root in concern for personal security, which still continues. When I was installed as Chief, I discussed the ceremony with the Bishop on the Niger (my diocesan bishop). There was only one part of the ceremony which presented difficulties and which we agreed I should not perform, and that was the ritualistic slaughter of a ram. My faith is perhaps more meaningful to me because I have had to think it through: I haven't just taken it for granted.

I am very comfortable being an Anglican: comfortable with the beliefs that Anglicanism represents, particularly the foundation of one common humanity. Belief in God motivates good human behaviour. Anglicanism cannot exclusively claim a belief in one God but, in my own part of the world, irrespective of colonialism, Anglicanism meant education and welfare and caring. It has given me a belief in the God whom we can approach through his Son, Jesus Christ.'

5

Matters of Life and Death

Elizabeth Butler-Sloss was called to the Bar in 1955 and became a High Court judge in 1979. In 1987/8 she chaired the Cleveland Child Abuse Inquiry, and from 1999 until her retirement in 2005 she was President of the Family Division. In 2002 she chaired the Crown Appointments Commission charged with the selection of a new Archbishop of Canterbury. She is Chairman of the Security Commission and Chancellor of the University of the West of England. She was appointed a Dame in 1979, a Privy Councillor in 1988 and a Dame Grand Cross in 2005.

'When our elder son was 15 and very clever and wanting to shock everybody, he said to me: "Justify why you're a Christian." I said I had absolutely no intention of letting him argue with me: this was my own personal belief. But I believe quite simply in the existence of God and the Trinity. I accept the teachings of the Church. I also believe that, having been born into God's world, God has responsibility for us but that that we have responsibility for our own individual actions.

I was born into an Anglican family: both my parents were from Norwich, which was in their time strongly Low Church Anglican. My mother told me that there were 47 Anglican churches in the city when she was young, and not a single Roman Catholic church until my grandfather, who was Sheriff of Norwich, persuaded the council to allow one to be built.

I was baptized into the Church of England, as were my three elder brothers. I was the only daughter, and it was expected that I would go to church with my mother, but it was not expected of my brothers or my father, who went on high days, such as Christmas Day and Easter Sunday. I stress the Low Church element because we went to St Luke's in Kew (we were living in Kew Gardens in Surrey) until there was a change of incumbent. The new vicar put a cross and candles on the altar, and my mother moved to St Anne's (on the Green), which was more Low Church.

My parents were not the sort of people who discussed things much with the children – certainly my mother did not. When I was grown up, my father and I discussed all sorts of things, but religion was not one of them. My mother had a totally unstated and I think very simple faith (which sustained her through a very difficult time, because she had MS for many years), and I just followed suit.

I went to Wycombe Abbey, which is a strongly Anglican school: straightforwardly middle-of-the-road C of E. Everybody had to go to chapel every day and twice on Sundays. (A great friend of mine at school was Jewish, and she ended up knowing far more about Anglicanism than most Christians, though she went to synagogue in the holidays.) I was confirmed in the school chapel, which was an uplifting experience, and I always enjoyed attending communion there.

When I left school, I went abroad for a year, which was splendidly hedonistic: I went to Lausanne University, took no exams, did no work and learned to speak good French with a bad accent. I was 17 and grew up very fast. Church didn't feature at all – I just went off and enjoyed myself.

Then I came back to the realities, which were that my mother by then was an invalid and my father had just been made a High Court judge, which meant he had to go out on circuit, sometimes for six or eight weeks. So I lived at home and studied for the Bar exams in London (from about the age of 12, when I went to Wycombe, I had decided I was going to be a barrister). I stayed at home in order to run the house; fortunately, we had enough help so I was extremely privileged in that I didn't have to do any of the hard work, but I was not as sympathetic to my mother as I should have been, and it was a difficult two or three years for both of us.

I met my husband at the Bar. He came from a very similar sort of background: he was an Ulsterman and was brought up in Bangor in County Down. His father was a solicitor in Belfast. Joe was a chorister at Bangor Abbey, and his sister and his mother (who was a pianist) also sang there.

Our daughter Frances was born twelve months after we were married, and we moved to live in the Temple. We became very friendly with the then Master of the Temple Church, Canon Milford (who was one of the founders of Oxfam), and that was a contributing factor to our attendance at the Temple Church. All three of our children and three of our grandchildren were baptized there. I feel strongly about the importance of baptism, which provides the child with the membership of the Church and the chance to belong to it in the deeper sense as an adult. If, later, the adult child does not wish to remain, s/he can choose to leave and a parent has no right to object, but the parents should give the child that choice. It is brave and not always easy to be baptized as an adult.

I have had no official politics for 35 years since I took my first judicial appointment, but before I was married I was involved in Young Conservative politics in London. A number of us agreed that, because we were living in totally safe Conservative constituencies, we would transfer to poorly supported constituencies in south London. That is how I went to Vauxhall and became chairman of the Young Conservatives (I think there were about eight members). As a result of that, I was asked to stand for the local elections and, subsequently, for parliament. So I did, and I loved it. I very, very much wanted to be a politician at the time and was envious of my brother who was elected some years later. I sometimes wonder how, if I had been elected, I would have dealt with some of the moral/ethical issues which arise. I am actually quite relieved that I was not put to the test and so did not have to struggle with my conscience.

In my many years on the Bench I was never faced with the dilemma of a conflict between my moral convictions and the decisions I had to make, even though in the last few years I made a number of difficult and potentially controversial decisions involving issues of legal and medical ethics. Although these decisions were not easy, I found the problems were mainly legal ones; the moral issues were, for me at least, entirely compatible with my own beliefs. I am sure that my understanding of what is fair and how people should be treated derives from my religious beliefs, which are compatible with the underlying moral dimension of the English common law, based as it is on Judaeo-Christian teaching.

I was occasionally unhappy about a result which I felt was unjust to a litigant. Sometimes (particularly when sitting with two other judges in the Court of Appeal), we said in our judgments that the legislation – or absence of legislation – in the case we were considering caused an unjust result and that the law should be changed. But we applied the existing law since it was our duty to do so. I might stretch the common law to encompass a new situation not covered by existing precedent or legislation, but I would never distort it. A well-known legal saying is that "hard cases make bad law". In our English practice of applying precedents to later cases, a decision which went outside the limits to accommodate one litigant might fall very harshly on a litigant in a subsequent case.

I did not agonize afterwards about the decisions I had to make, though I worried from time to time before I made a decision about what the result should be. I saw my appointment as a judge as a duty which took precedence over my personal beliefs: I did not have the right to pick and choose the law I applied according to my views as an individual. It might have been more difficult had I been a Roman Catholic, since some decisions involved the removal of artificial nutrition and hydration from patients in a permanent vegetative state, which led inevitably to their death; there were other life-or-death decisions too, and occasionally a decision required the approval of contraception or abortion for a teenager.

Several high-profile cases have involved the balance between the sanctity of life and personal autonomy. Two examples are Miss B, who was rendered paralysed and did not want to be kept alive on an artificial ventilator, and Mrs Diane Pretty, who was a motor-neurone victim who was not being artificially kept alive; consequently, if her husband helped her to die he was in danger of being prosecuted.

Mrs Pretty wanted her husband to give her something to bring her life to an end. If he did so he would be guilty of assisting her to commit suicide. She was able to stay alive without requiring artificial breathing or feeding and her request was turned down by all the courts, including the European Court of Human Rights. What Miss B wanted was to be taken off the artificial ventilator – her view was that she should never have been put on it, and therefore she

51

was requiring the doctors to turn it off. Since Miss B was kept alive artificially and was competent to refuse medical treatment she was entitled to come off the artificial ventilator. Miss B was a Pentecostal Christian and the saddest aspect of her case was her loss of faith as a result of her devastating injury. She was a most impressive person and I hoped that she might decide to stay alive to be an example to others. She chose to die.

The case of Mrs Pretty was very sad, but I feel strongly that there is a great danger in allowing assisted suicides and accepting the principle of euthanasia. I do so for two reasons. The first is that there would inevitably be a degree of pressure, however discreetly applied, to many old people who live reasonably happy though restricted lives and are, by the fact of their continuing existence, using up the assets which would otherwise be inherited by their families. The second is that I have profound belief that we were given our lives by God and that we should live our allotted span, whatever period that might be. When I am dying, I would certainly be grateful not to have my life prolonged and I do not want to be resuscitated. If I am in pain, I would hope to be given morphine; if it were necessary to administer it to a degree which shortened my life, I would be very relieved. However, actually to make a decision to bring my life to an end is, I believe, morally wrong. I don't believe a Christian should do that.

It would not cross my mind not to be an Anglican: the Church of England is part of my life. However, if it were to join with the Church of Rome, I would find it extraordinarily difficult to know what to do: I could not accept papal infallibility, nor a ban on priests marrying, nor a ban on women priests. I was, to begin with, very opposed to women priests. I suspect it was a basic feminine feeling that

I did not want to be lectured at from the pulpit by a woman. And then I pulled myself together and recognized what a very superficial approach that was; there seemed to be no genuine theological reason why women couldn't be ordained as priests. I think quite often people look to theology to back up their emotional feelings. So I came to the conclusion that I had no right to object, and I think that women have added enormously to the Church. It follows from that that I do not see how there can be a rational objection to women bishops.

The question of gay priests seems to me to be much more difficult and it raises two different sorts of issues. The first is: is there a fundamental theological objection to gays and lesbians being accepted as members of the Church? If the Church said that there was then I feel I would have to accept it, but I would be very concerned about the injustice to those who do not conform to a heterosexual way of life. As I understand the arguments, only some members of the Church take that stand.

It is important to recognize that the secular approach to homosexuality has changed dramatically in the last few years and the passing of the Civil Partnership Bill has transformed the recognition of stable homosexual relationships. It is a flagship Act, because it provides a legal framework and a just solution for those who make a serious commitment to a partner but cannot have that partnership recognized as marriage. I should be very opposed to such a relationship being called marriage, but these relationships can no longer be ignored. For the Church to ignore them is to exclude a section of society which is recognized by the State and has much to offer to the community. Some of these relationships have children, either of one partner or, under our new legislation, adopted by both gay partners. To treat all these people as unable to be part of the Church community is in modern times unrealistic and will, in my view, rebound on the Church more than upon the individuals. It would seem to follow that recognition of the position of gays and lesbians in the community would lead to the ordination of clergy from that section of society.

The second issue, however, is that there is a distinction to be drawn between recognition and public acceptance. I am sure it will be much easier for the public to accept a woman bishop than gay or lesbian priests openly living with their partners. One of the great strengths of the Church of England is its emphasis on evolution rather than revolution, and I feel that we have to be cautious for totally pragmatic reasons. The problem is, of course, for how long?

Cohabitation without marriage has now become normal but is not included in the Cohabitation Act. I can see that it is now sensible for people to live together before marriage: much more realistic, in fact, to do that than to get divorced because they have married too quickly. It is a sensible compromise. But I believe it's wrong in principle for people to live together on a long-term basis and to have children without marrying. I also believe that marriage is for life, although I have helped to divorce a lot of people: the civil law provides for divorce and I did not believe it was part of my job to tell people (who may or may not be Christians) that they should not get divorced.

I have found being Chairman of the Advisory Council of St Paul's Cathedral an absolutely fascinating job (it's also great fun: I don't allow Council meetings to be too serious). I see it as, in a very small way, paying back something from which I have had such benefit. I find St Paul's inspirational. I like beautiful things and I like the services. I very much like Cathedral Evensong at 5 p.m. When I'm chairing the Council, if I possibly can, I go to Evensong beforehand because it gives me a moment just to sit and gather my thoughts.

When we are in London we go regularly to the Temple Church and I feel very much at home there. It is much easier to go to church in London than in the country, where we are almost always without a regular parson, and we have to get the car out to go to another village. My relationship with the Church in the country is very largely one of guilt: I know that the Church is not a private matter and that we are part of the community and should be joining in. I feel I am spoiled by the beauty of the services I go to in London. I falter in the country.

I derive profound pleasure, in the deepest sense, from going to a service where I am at home and comfortable, know my way around the service and understand it. If I go to a church where I have to keep flipping over the pages and wondering where I am, I find it much more difficult to concentrate and therefore I get less value from it. That, for me, is what is marvellous about Prayer Book services: I do not need to open the Prayer Book at the communion service except to read the epistle and the gospel.

I have come to terms with the new service-book, and I appreciate why we have it. I do exchange the Peace, because I do not want to offend, but for preference I would rather not. I am all for enthusiasm, but cautious about the enthusiasm which turns into over-enthusiasm, or even hysteria. I would find it difficult to stand up in church or in public and talk about coming closer to God. I am not very good at fervency.

Having been marvellously busy in my working life, I have never really reflected very much on what I think; I tend to feel what I do, rather than intellectualize it. I am instinctively a Christian. I have never felt (as I know some people do feel), a sense of direct communication with God, but I do have a real sense, on a regular basis, of what I should or should not do. When issues arise which have to be resolved I do ask for help through prayer and then, if I have time, I let the problem rest and think it over in the bath, or bed, or wherever I am, and then leave it, because generally I shall know sooner or later what I ought to do. So the way I live my life is largely instinctive, but I feel I gain real help from time to time, whether or not it is actually an answer to my prayer. In my personal life I have a considerable degree of self-doubt and guilt, because I know that I fail most of the time in what I set myself.

Nothing I have said has any effect on whether or not I remain an Anglican. One of the joys of the Church of England is that we belong to such a broad Church that I can believe things that I know my neighbour may not believe. That should be a strength for the members, but sadly it does not appear at present to be so. My understanding of being an Anglican has given me the freedom to carry out my life in the law without restriction, but supported by my beliefs and by the help that member-ship of the Church has given me over the years.

I do not believe we are entitled to certainty but I do want a church that is open – in every sense of the word – when I need to think, and is there to help me when I fail, and to remind me of my duty to God.'

6

Building on the Past

Frank Field *has been MP for Birkenhead since 1979. Before winning that seat he was Director of the Child Poverty Action Group. He was Minister for Welfare Reform in the early days of the Blair government. He has been a co-opted member of General Synod and he now chairs the Churches' Conservation Trust and the Cathedrals' Fabric Commission for England.*

'I've always been an Anglican. I cannot therefore claim any great conversion experience, and I feel deprived as a result. I think it's wonderful to be with people who talk of a personal relationship with Jesus, but I can only say that for me, on balance, believing the story makes more sense than not doing so.

I had a typically English Christian upbringing in that it was one without any rigorous teaching, yet it was sacramental. One of the weaknesses of Anglicanism is that it isn't now good at grounding its adherents doctrinally. I remain an Anglican, partly because that's where I was born and it seems reasonable to stay there, and partly because, for want of a better word, I have strongly sympathetic gut-feelings for the Church of England. The famous quip that "The Anglican Church knows how much the English will take of religion – which is not very much" holds a great truth

57

about the English character and emphasizes how much the form of the Anglican Church is a product of our culture.

The traditional Anglican mindset is based on the understanding that truth can be many-sided, that it's sensible to look at Scripture and to adhere to tradition, but above all to use our conscience in matters of interpreting our faith so we form some kind of a daily highway code. The central attraction of Anglicanism for me is that it has a New Testament approach. Jesus very rarely gave any answers; instead, he turned questions round and (in effect) asked: "What do you think?" The Anglican Church is faithful to that approach: "Here is the background; here is what scripture says; this is how previous generations have interpreted those truths – now you decide." There are those wonderful lines from R.S. Thomas:

> I have abandoned
> my theories, the easier certainties
> of my belief. There are no handrails to grasp.[1]

Anglican ritual at its best is very difficult to beat and it does in its essence symbolize something that is beyond us, as does the rhythm of our services. The liturgy gives meaning and shape to our lives. Yet the wider changes in our society are now reflected in the Church, and not always for the better. Take the common courtesies, for example. We're much more likely to talk before the service: we've lost the sense of preparation for something that cannot be fully understood. The sense of awe and mystery is being eroded. It is a big loss.

As children, we were taken to St Nicholas in Chiswick by my mother. It was, I would say, low church Catholic – sacramental without any obsession with church millinery. In later life I've developed a great passion for Pearson churches, and it's only very recently that I've found out that St Nicholas is a Pearson church (he didn't build the tower, so he didn't bother to list the building). Pearson, more than any other Victorian architect, captures space brilliantly. R.S. Thomas, if I may quote him again, describes it thus:

Often I try
To analyse the quality
Of its silences. Is this where God hides
From my searching?[2]

It's important for anyone growing up in this country, and wanting to understand it, to know something about Christianity. People may want to reject it all as hocus-pocus but, unless we know about it in the first place, we can't make a choice. Knowledge about faith is, of course, different from faith itself. Faith is a gift, but I hope I don't sound too flippant if I say that knowledge about our faith appears to make the Holy Spirit's job somewhat easier. Certainly it's clear that, if we do the groundwork, the Holy Spirit at least finds it easier to impart the gifts than if we do nothing at all. There is nothing in Scripture to support the view that we should sit back, take the easy option and simply allow the Church's decline to continue.

Where best might we transmit that knowledge about our faith? It is, of course, in schools, and we should be concentrating as much of our energy as possible in them. Not only is the school a place in which one can teach something about the faith, but there is also another opportunity here. If you take my constituency of Birkenhead, for example, all too many families simply don't function, and school is the one part of life which, despite all the shortcomings, provides a sense of stability for children. That makes school a place in which one could certainly teach something about the faith. I think as a church we should be much more serious about capitalizing on the advantages the State offers us.

We have taken for granted in this country that families would function well and that, as a result, people naturally become social animals. We're learning to our cost that this no longer occurs automatically. What's increasingly happening is that a larger and larger number of children are to a greater or lesser extent out of control. Some of their parents are unaware of what's been happening to their children, while others are out of control themselves. You see it at all levels of society, but it's worst for the poor because they can't escape from the horrors of this as those of us with bank balances can.

From the early 1800s (and maybe before that), as people moved to towns in greater numbers, there was a real effort by ordinary people to become involved in the march towards respectability. For a century or more, we've benefited from families teaching the basic common decencies. What successful families have done is to accept that all of us are born with original sin and that each of us thereby views ourselves as the centre of the world. Then, if we are lucky, the family gently introduces us to the fact that four or five other people are also the centre of the world. By reconciling those apparently contradictory positions, and developing a sense of give and take, families that function well help to school each of us for the wider world.

Bound up with this great march to respectability was the Christian faith. Even those who couldn't believe still hoped that Christian morality would survive without an underpinning of Christian dogma. We have tested that theory to destruction. For a long time it looked as if the morality side would survive. Events now suggest otherwise. Worse still, we are now at a stage where traditional Christian language, instead of being a purveyor of meaning, is a barrier: how do you convey the great truths when most people have no idea what you're talking about?

It seems to me that the Church has two tasks: one is to give people the confidence to discern between what is right and what is wrong in everyday life. Then there are the new issues which are focused by the advance of science, which raise the very essence of what we now mean by "life".

I'm part of the parliamentary group for Dying Well. When we're fighting euthanasia bills, or more specifically during the Mental Capacity Bill (which started as the Mental Incapacity Bill), the perception in the House of Commons is that the Church is totally unconcerned about how people die and that "life" should take its course whatever the consequences. Given the Christian belief about the afterlife this is, to put it mildly, a cruel paradox. In fact, of course, Church teaching is that we shouldn't strive officiously to keep somebody alive. Dying, and the importance of dying well, is one area where we should have a distinctive contribution to make; another is to the debate about what constitutes life, and what protection there should be for it. So we need a church which can engage intellectually with these sorts of issues, while also operating effectively at a parish and school level in conveying something about God. At this level of activity the Church's influence will so often depend upon the quality of the person concerned, rather than the words which are used: there are people who touch our lives simply because of who they are in themselves.

As England's social cohesion continues to disintegrate, the Church has a vital contribution to make to the debate about the nature and the rearing of children, for here is the root of our present discontent. It becomes increasingly important that the Church should have the confidence to express its views, not in a condemnatory way, but to show what we stand for and why we hold these views. Again it comes back to tradition. What does past experience show? What message is it trying to give? So, while it is marvellous to give place to diversity, societies do not survive by endlessly and only emphasizing diversity: there have to be core values to which people automatically subscribe. How do we hold these two standpoints together? Let me illustrate this with respect to the family.

It ought to be possible for us to say, without having a vendetta against single mothers, that we do think it's better for children to have two parents who live together, and that's the norm to which we want people to aspire. Currently, for all too many young people growing up in Birkenhead, that is not the norm. If we are not prepared to offer any guidance as to what the ground-rules are, why should we expect anyone to keep them?

Again, we should be making a distinction between, on the one hand, couples who – for whatever reason – grow apart, and on the other the rise of the very young single mother who, for all intents and purposes, is still a child herself. Do we serve this person's needs best by pretending she is an adult with all the rights which accompany adult status? And what about the rights of the new-born child? Or are we going to be brave enough to say that children are best nurtured in families of two parents and lots of grandparents; that it is massively difficult for mothers on their own to raise children, although some do incredibly well? And shouldn't this view be reflected in the range of help offered? Should everyone, for example, have automatic access to independent housing? Above all, what moves do we intend to make to ensure that young fathers remain a crucial part of the life of this baby?

As a society, all too many of us have forgotten the great truth about how important the early years are for the kind of adults children will become. Our current system, for example, allows mothers to pay somebody else to look after their children, but not to claim anything for doing it themselves. How sensible is this? As a society we now share much more fairly the cost of raising children and we do this primarily through child benefit and the tax-credit system. We are spending £100,000 per child up to the age of 19. Shouldn't we think how this sum might be better spent by giving parents greater choice in when they draw down part of this sum? Wouldn't it be better, say, to allow mothers (and it will be mainly mothers) to claim £25,000 of this sum (which comes tax-free) so that they can concentrate on being mothers for the first two years of their child's life? Of course there are exceptions, but most mothers will look after their own children better than other people will.

Here is a role for the Church as a teaching body. There are only so many times that its leaders will be reported (and can thereby teach) by stressing the need for children to be brought up, wherever possible, by two parents who live together. It might have been appropriate at the time of William Temple for the Church to deal (as it was called) in middle axioms. But we were a different society then. Such an approach now doesn't cut much ice in the wider political debate. The hierarchy has to have members who can hold their own in the detailed policy prescriptions of everyday politics. There are a couple of bishops who do just this in respect of the countryside.

Similarly, the Church has to see how it can get ahead of the game by imaginatively thinking about secularizing some of its own rituals, believing, as I do, that these rituals developed because they served a general as well as a particular need. Again, let me give you one example.

When the British Expeditionary Force went to France in 1914, 99 per cent of them were baptized. Of the troops that went to Iraq, fewer than 40 per cent were baptized. As the Church withdraws, or becomes more marginalized, it's important for the community to maintain the universality of these rituals. For instance, initiation is important for the welcoming of an individual into our wider society. Shouldn't the Church therefore be at the forefront in a campaign to make registering the birth of a child a public ceremony, as a way of welcoming a baby into the wider community, beyond their immediate family (as baptism once was)? Shouldn't we say that it is through this public ceremony that families gain entry into child benefit, and that with the privileges of child benefit come certain duties? Here would be an opportunity to say, "This is what the resources are that society is committing to each child, and in return here are the duties that we believe you as parents will want to carry out." This approach need not undermine Christian initiation: just as Anglican priests are also registrars, so they would be able to conduct these initiation ceremonies – but other organizations would as well.

Another opportunity would be the equivalent of a bar mitzvah. Here society should lift another ritual and universalize it. We badly need a rite of passage which helps children realize they are ceasing to be a child and are on the threshold of adulthood. Shouldn't such a ritual be part of the schools' curriculum and weighted accordingly?

Throughout the whole of our history we've had an extraordinary tension between being an episcopal Church and also one in which the laity are extremely important in running things. The loss by the Church Commissioners of large sums of money is only now being fully felt. The balance between bishops as leaders and teachers, and the laity, has been significantly changed by the financial weakness of the Commissioners. The income from the Commissioners' assets provided a crucial buffer against the fads which tend to capture the laity. This is now less true: the faddists know that they have the upper hand. Money from the parishes is now much more important than it ever was for financing those central functions that any Church must undertake. We saw self-righteousness parading itself on stilts over the Jeffrey John affair, with some laity threatening to withhold payment of their parish quota.

Part of being Anglican has meant paying up even when one disagreed with what was happening, trusting that in time all of us will have a clearer view of what truth is. The generosity of this approach has allowed the Church to incorporate a breadth of belief wherein truth may hide. We are now much more party-ridden, and those with the money more determined than ever to call the tune. Although it was ever thus, in the past the Commissioners' assets provided a bulwark against such bullying. It is a terrible sight to see people so possessed of what they believe to be the truth combining such certainty with an unforgiving and unbending will. This growing financial weakness of the Commissioners (growing because I believe we will have to revalue what proportion of the historic assets will finally have to be made over to past pension promises) takes the Anglican Church into new territory.

You can't understand England without understanding the role of the Church, and you can't understand the Church without beginning to understand why people constructed so many beautiful churches. We now face the real likelihood in the not-too-distant future of many congregations being no longer able to maintain all of these wonderful buildings. I do think it ought to be possible for us to devise ways in which those of us in this country who love

English churches, and what they stand for, can contribute directly towards the cost of maintaining them, thereby ensuring their future. The Bishop of London has opened up the discussion on how more churches can be held by local trusts. Some people find this rather novel, even shocking. But it is, in effect, a reactionary move in the real sense of that word. That is how the local community used to regard the nave of the church – as theirs, for them to carry out whatever business they thought suitable to undertake there. We need to capture the best of past practice when thinking about the future.'

NOTES

1. R.S. Thomas, 'Balance', from *Frequencies* (London: Macmillan, 1978).
2. R.S. Thomas, 'In Church', from *Pieta* (London: Rupert Hart Davis, 1966).

7

Faith and Work

Andreas Whittam Smith *is First Church Estates Commissioner and responsible for over £4 billion of church investments. He was originally a financial journalist and launched the* Independent, *where he was the founder editor. Since stepping down as editor, he has been President of the British Board of Film Censorship and Chairman of the Financial Ombudsman Service. He remains a non-executive director of the* Indie *and writes a weekly column. He and his wife divide their time between London and Paris.*

'I am an extreme example of the taciturn Englishman so far as speaking about my faith is concerned. I was born an Anglican; it's part of my DNA.

My father was a vicar in the Chester diocese throughout my formative years. In 1940 we moved from the safe countryside around Macclesfield near Manchester, to Birkenhead on Merseyside, just a week or two before the Germans started bombing the neighbouring ports and shipyards. Our church was a landmark for enemy aircraft, and my memories of that time include sheltering in the cellar and my father having to bury huge numbers of people when an entire street was wiped out.

On Merseyside nowadays there is an upside-down game of social point-scoring: the winner is the person who can prove that he or she was brought up in the poorest area. I have a very high card: my little bit of Birkenhead beats almost all others for deprivation, boarded-up houses and general misery.

Like all teenage boys, I was in mild rebellion against my father (without knowing that he was actually already seriously ill with the cancer from which he eventually died). But our disputes weren't about religion: Church was life as it was, and faith was an unquestioned assumption. I can't say I had a conversion experience: I didn't, nor do I feel deprived as a result.

My mother and father worked equally hard in the Church: they were a church couple. My mother had been teaching the piano in London before she met my father when he became the vicar of her parents' parish in Macclesfield. When they married, she gave up her work until she was widowed, when she took it up again to earn some money. In between she worked full-time as a clergy wife, running the Mothers' Union, doing everything – it was very much as if it was a grocer's shop, only it happened to be a church. All the family were involved: my jobs were pulling the bell, counting the collection, putting out the hymn books, singing in the choir, and so on. That is why I feel completely comfortable in churches, whereas a lot of people don't.

At school I was affected by that ceaseless teasing which says, if you do anything wrong, "Oh, you're a vicar's son", and I do wonder if that's the explanation for my extreme reluctance to talk about my faith. I also used to get bullied on my way to school: big lads would set on me, though they never really did me any harm. But I would scamper from the scene as fast as I could. I had learned very early in life a lesson that I employed once more as a student, while working in a restaurant kitchen with a violent chef, that discretion is the better part of valour.

My school was in effect a grammar school of the direct grant-aided type: a good school of its kind, but it was intellectually snobbish. It was decided early on that I wasn't going to get an Oxbridge scholarship and was therefore of no use whatsoever. This decision riled me. I used to inhabit the local public library in Birkenhead, where I often looked at reference books. One day I saw a little blue-backed book called *The Statutes of Oxford University*. When I read it, I discovered that scholars were quite a small part of Oxford's intake and most students were what used to be called Commoners: they had to take an entrance exam.

I decided to have a go, but the individual colleges were a complete mystery to me. I ran my finger down the list and read about each one until I came to Keble, which I learned was a Church of England foundation and that the Warden was a clergyman. So I thought, "That's the one for me", because, with a little bit of luck, my father might conjure a reference out of the bishop – which he did. So I took the exam without breathing a word of it to the school, and when I got the letter offering a place, I told them I was going to Oxford. At first they were appalled, and then they thought they'd better stop being appalled.

I had a long period of failure in my life. The first failure was in not being selected for the scholarship class; the second was when, before going up to Oxford, I went into the army to do my national service. If you had any education at all, it was assumed that you should be an officer so you went up to something called the War Office Selection Board to be tested for initiative. Typically, you would be given a plank six feet wide and asked to get your men across a river that was twelve feet across. I managed that, and then I did something which I know was characteristic, and I'd probably do again. I thought that, having solved the problem, the best thing was to merge into the background. I'd succeeded in the task and didn't want to stand out and perhaps ruin my success.

At the end, the Brigadier said he'd been observing me and he could see that I wasn't fit to lead men because, once I'd succeeded at something, I relaxed and made no further effort. So he condemned me to the ranks – whereupon one of my permanent rules of life came into play, which is "If you're not at the top, you've got to be at the bottom." I sank like a stone to the depths of the British army and spent two years with what you might call the lads on the football terraces.

Then I went up to Oxford. I hadn't realized that it would still be *Brideshead Revisited*. It was incredibly social, and at first I felt very uneasy amongst lots of public-schoolboy types. But towards the end of my first term I acquired a girlfriend who was herself well-connected and came from this upper-class area of life which was completely foreign to me – it might as well have been Mongolia as far as I was concerned. Then I discovered in myself a not very admirable ability to be a chameleon, and I fitted in to such an extent that I soon found myself being invited to all the big social occasions. I did very little work, and there was a horrible moment at the end of my course when the class list was pinned up and I discovered to my deepest horror that I'd got a Third. I was absolutely disgusted with myself, but it changed my life: I've worked hard ever since.

I discovered that I like working. I enjoy it and I've now reached the very luxurious position where I make no distinction between work and leisure. Retirement is not an option. I really would rather stack supermarket shelves than not work. I feel very strongly that you must contribute something, and that's part of a work ethic which is deeply and utterly Protestant.

As a clergyman, my father stood on the Equator, so to speak – in the very middle. He was neither high nor low church, and that's where I remain to this day, although the middle ground seems to be vanishing. My churchgoing is 8 a.m. communion in the Book of Common Prayer version. If I still had a young family it would be different, because I think family services are a good thing. I'm married to a Roman Catholic, so my children had a partly Catholic upbringing.

My wife and I are currently trying to achieve two-city living. We don't say that we live in Paris and have somewhere in London, or the other way round: we live in London and Paris. We alternate between three wonderful Catholic churches close to us in Paris. (I've never even been to the Anglican Church.) One is St Germain de Près (I'm always moved by churches of a historic nature and that's the earliest church in Paris, about AD 550). Another is St Sulpice, which is the major church after Notre Dame – huge, very well-staffed, with a superb organist. Both of these churches have cosmopolitan congregations. And then round the corner from us is St Thomas d'Aquin, which is very much a French family church. We probably go to St Thomas more than the other two. The last time we were there, I was reflecting on the Anglican Communion and I thought to myself that I'm not deeply concerned about the unity of the Church. There was a lovely service, very well conducted, very full congregation, lots of families – and, equally, everything was completely recognizable to me. Even if I didn't know French I'd know where I was in the Mass because the rhythm tells me – it could have been in Spanish or Romanian.

To me, St Mary Abbots (where I worship in London) and St Thomas d'Aquin are obviously part of one universal Church. But when I'm in France I won't take communion. I know that, if I wanted to, I should speak to the priest and most likely he'd say, "Yes, you can." But a Protestant bit of me niggles here: if the Pope won't recognize Anglican orders, I'm not going to take communion in one of his churches. There's very little that's displeasing to me in the Roman Catholic Church in Paris, except the singing, which is deplorable.

I'm struck by the restraint of the French Catholic Church – I've not yet smelt incense in Paris. If you go to Ireland or Italy, that's Roman Catholicism flat out, full on. French Catholicism is close to Anglicanism; we're both secular countries and the figures showing the numbers of church-goers tend to be about the same, despite the different confessions.

There was a time when I was young when, though I didn't lose my faith (which has been strong throughout my life), my churchgoing became less regular. That period lasted until I was 25, perhaps 27 – then I went back to my regular habit. But the bedrock of my spiritual life is undoubtedly private prayer. It is very, very important to me – probably more important than going to church. I need physical exercise and spiritual exercise and I do quite a bit of both. In praying, I have a framework (I'm a great lover of form). I follow a long programme which I invented for myself and which is just as elaborate as the Catholic rosary.

The whole of British society is suffused with Judaeo-Christian moral standards. We don't know we have them, but we do. Fewer and fewer people grow up knowing the Christian story, but they observe the teaching. So I think it's very difficult to tease out what difference faith makes in the workplace, and I find it particularly hard when I see the way in which Christian people conduct themselves within the bosom of the Church of England. I'm very struck by the fact that people inside the Church treat each other more unkindly than I have ever seen in Fleet Street, or indeed in any other walk of life.

When I was in charge at the British Board of Film Censors, the faith–work issue could have been acute. I was lucky that my period in office went by without one of those films that occasionally come along which actually mock Christianity – I'd have found that very hard to deal with. But I'm permanently on the brink (and one day I'll go over the brink) of protesting to the Advertising Standards Authority about advertisements which use the imagery of the Last Supper. I don't see why my religion should be mocked. But I suppose the main thing about the film board was that ultimately everything came down to a series of simple ethical questions.

Everything about my present job as First Church Estates Commissioner has been a colossal surprise. The picture of the Church that I carried around in my head before starting was still the image I had derived from my father's vicarage. Going to the little church in Hampstead, where Richard Harries (later Bishop of Oxford) was my vicar, or attending St Mary Abbots in Kensington (as I have done for the past 25 years) didn't alter that image, and from the pew I could never have imagined how the Church works at the top.

I suppose the greatest shock was to find how weak are the authority levels in all parts of the Church, and I think that's one of the reasons why the national press tend to misunderstand the Church: they can't grasp that it isn't run by anybody, although the moral authority of the Archbishops is very great. I want the bishops to lead; the Archbishops' Council should be merely an executive branch of the House of Bishops.

I don't like the bishops challenging the Archbishops in public, if only by implication. Given that the Church of

England is an excessively democratic institution with a synodical system and every possible opportunity for people to make their points privately, I think it's very self-indulgent to go public and write to the papers.

Twenty years ago, I was City Editor of the *Daily Telegraph*. I read in the news one morning that somebody I'd never heard of called Eddie Shah was going to launch a new tabloid national newspaper called *Today* and I thought: what a crazy thing to do. Then I started to think a bit more deeply about Shah's initiative. The factors which had led him to do this were quite important and profound, and I thought: maybe it's not crazy at all.

So I dreamed up the notion of launching a new quality broadsheet, to be called *The Independent*. There are a couple of times in your life when you can take big risks: one is when you're in your twenties and you don't yet have a family, and another is when you're the age I was then (late forties), when your children have either finished or very nearly finished their schooling. So Valerie and I felt that if it all went wrong we wouldn't be able to help with university but still they'd probably make out. The crucial thing with risk-taking is that you should look over the cliff-edge and fully contemplate the worst that could happen and ask yourself whether you could cope. Could you accept the dire consequences of failure and make a new life for yourself? If yes, then proceed. But never look down again. So I took the decision to get on with the *Independent,* and after that it was like crossing a thousand bridges – so many crucial things to be solved before you got to the launch.

It wasn't primarily a money thing (as long as we did well for our shareholders). The driving force was very much the belief that there was a better way of doing journalism and we really could be independent. That's why all the rules were so strict, like no freebies and not covering Royal Family tittle-tattle. More importantly, we were innovators. We had an education page in the beginning, and an architecture page; we did health – these things had never been done before. You can't launch something new without at least 20 unique selling points, which we had. Within a year, all of Fleet Street had copied our ideas.

We also had two simple rules, which were revolutionary at the time: respect the reader; trust the writer. Respecting the reader is different from being popular, and means you're never going to patronize the reader or dumb down. Trusting the writer means you don't tell writers what to say before they start their piece; if you don't trust somebody, don't employ him or her.

The result of this was a very successful paper for quite a long time and then, of course, as often happens, we lost our way for a variety of reasons. I could give you a list of 20 mistakes I made: big mistakes, mainly to do with doing too much myself, misunderstanding colour and starting the *Independent on Sunday*, which I'm very proud of but which was a mistake because it took too much away from the daily paper. We invented Saturday: we were the first people to have a Saturday magazine. Most of what you see in Fleet Street today was invented in the *Independent* in 1987.

Thanks to my mother, I'm fluent in two languages: one is English and the other is music. In my early thirties I decided I was going to have a second bash at the piano and see how good I could get. I worked very hard with a good teacher and then I came to the edge of the great gap which divides the amateur from the professional. It was exactly like looking across from the Scottish mainland to the Isle of Mull: there's a dangerous, unbridgeable gulf and you can't get across.

I love church music: not only Anglican music, but Schubert Masses and the old things that are hardly sung any longer, like Stainer's *Crucifixion*. My sister lives in Montpellier, which is an old Protestant area of France, where they have *temples* and they still sing all the old German Reformation hymns. Singing those was a very pleasing experience, which made me see that the Protestant and the Catholic parts of Anglicanism really do fit well together.

I shall never desert Anglicanism, even if I'm the last man left standing on the bridge as the ship goes down – there's nothing that could drive me out. There are three things I might be prepared to die for: I'd die for my Church, I'd die for my country and I'd die for my family.

If I had to give a picture of my role now as First Church Estates Commissioner, such as it is, I'd liken myself to the keeper of the theatre. My job is to sweep the stage, count the money, switch the lights on – just as I was brought up to do in my parents' vicarage, only now on a larger scale. I'm never going to be on the stage myself – I don't have that gift. I've not been called. My task is to help to keep the show on the road. It's not an unworthy calling, and I'm very happy doing it – as long as I'm not the person who, at the end of the show, has to turn off the lights as the last person leaves. That would be a pity.'

8

Hearing the Call

Stephen Layton is a conductor. His interpretations of Bach and Handel have been heard from the Sydney Opera House to the Concertgebouw and with orchestras from the Academy of Ancient Music to the London Philharmonic and the Philadelphia. He founded Polyphony in 1986, and has made première recordings of Britten, Part, Tavener, Adès and Macmillan. He has worked with many choirs, holding positions as Chief Conductor of the Netherlands Chamber Choir, Chief Guest Conductor of the Danish Radio Choir and Director of the Holst Singers. As Director of Music at the Temple Church, he premièred Tavener's all-night vigil, The Veil of the Temple, *in London and New York. In September 2006 he becomes Director of Music and Fellow of Trinity College, Cambridge.*

'I made something close to a conscious choice of Anglicanism when I was just 11 or 12 and had been a choirboy at Winchester Cathedral for a couple of years. I had been brought up as an evangelical in the Elim Pentecostal church in Derby, where my father was the organist. As a little boy I went with my parents to all the Sunday services, morning and evening. When I was about 9, I started to play the piano in church (there was a tradition that piano and organ played together).

I was often uncomfortable in the sermons (or the Word as we called it) because, as a small boy, I found the style frightening. The voice of the preacher was raised and, especially when we had a visiting American preacher, things were invariably wound up into a frenzied tempo. It was generally the evening service that was the most passionate, and it usually culminated in asking you to give your life to Christ. This was always after I had had tea with my granny, and I remember it being a particular struggle to digest the fiery preaching on a stomach full of cakes.

A positive side of Elim was that I discovered the power of music to transform the experience of worship and to lift the worshipper into another state, whether of awe, wonder or simply contemplation. This was formative in influencing my later experience as an Anglican. It created in me a natural expectation that any service of worship should foster an awareness of the Holy Spirit, leaving one open to the unexpected. The power of music in that Derby church was remarkable. During "prayer time" somebody might start to sing a chorus softly, and gradually everybody would join in. Either my father or I (usually me, because I had perfect pitch) would find the right key for their singing. Somehow, with no written music, we would manage to play the same harmonies for songs such as "How Great Thou Art". The very first time this happened it completely took me away because, by the end of the singing, everyone was on their feet with their arms in the air. So, although as a small boy I was disturbed by the preaching style, it seemed to me to be a pretty good thing that people were rejoicing and celebrating what they believed through music. This deeply personal sense that I was worshipping as I sang, and that this was a way of being changed or of being open to change, has never left me.

Through all this musical experience in that Elim church my own musical gifts flourished. Even at the age of 9, I would sometimes do the "Ministry in Song" slot on a Sunday night. This involved getting up onto the dais in church in front of 600 people. I would sing and my father would accompany and afterwards the minister would pray and say, "Isn't the Lord wonderful how he's given Stephen the gift?" So I was very aware that I could sing! My father was an organist who had taught himself the piano (in his teens, he had paid for piano lessons by doing a paper-round). He was a big influence because he got me going on the keyboard from very young and gave me huge encouragement.

Although they realized that I could sing, my parents were not really familiar with the cathedral tradition. It was a musical friend of my father's, visiting from Australia, who suggested that I should be a chorister and found out where there were voice-trials. Winchester Cathedral offered me a place. For about six months before I went to Winchester, my father sent me to sing on Sunday nights in St John's, an Anglo-Catholic church in Derby. He sensibly thought that this would help me to bridge the gap between the totally different traditions of the Elim Church and Winchester Cathedral. It was certainly made clear to me that it would be a big adjustment. Just before leaving Derby, I remember the minister at Elim taking me aside and praying with me that God would protect me, which I took to mean protecting me from bowing to the altar and praying to Mary in clouds of incense. (In fact, when I arrived at Winchester there was little, if any, incense, and I certainly wasn't struck by "popish" practices!) The experience at St John's was particularly helpful in introducing me to structure. The Elim services were structured in the way that a brilliant speech-maker jots down ten headings: we had the Word, the Ministry in Song, hymns and prayer times, but it was all pretty flexible. So it was the formal structure of the prescribed forms of service that was one of the first things that hit me about the Church of England.

I liked it immediately. I liked the order of it. But the main thing that thrilled me was that I was singing wonderful music and, through the power of this music, I felt I was somehow being spoken to. The very first morning of boys' practice in Winchester (it would have been something like 8 January 1976, at 8.15 in the practice room in the Pilgrims' School, in the Tudor Priory buildings), we sang a scale or two and then the cathedral organist, Martin Neary, put the chords down for the opening of S.S. Wesley's "Ascribe unto the Lord" and we all came in with, "Let the whole earth stand in awe of him". I was next to one of the senior boys (the little ones sat either side of the seniors) so I got the full roar of the boy singing and it just bowled me over, so much so that I remember it to this day. We worked on that first phrase, "Let the whole earth stand in awe of him", and I made the connection that what we were talking about was something awesome, and that this Being you were standing in awe of was absolutely out there. Probably because the quality of the music was so high, it suddenly seemed as if this was the real thing. After the fire and brimstone of Elim, I was quite frightened of God, but this seemed to be a dignified, wonderful way of acknowledging his presence and celebrating it with the best that you could offer. That attracted me. Perhaps because of my musical acuity, I wanted the music to be amazing. There had certainly been times in the Elim church when I had felt that the spirit was strong but the music was sloppy. It was as though I had now encountered something that Elim had pointed towards. Suddenly to be experiencing the greatest music of the Church of England was, for me as a small boy, exciting beyond anything I had known. Looking back, it was the turning-point.

And it was the best. Both the Dean, Michael Stancliffe, and the Bishop, John V. Taylor, were extraordinarily involved in the music, working closely with the organist, Martin Neary. As choristers, we realized how important the music was to all of them. I discerned no tension and there was always a sense of solidarity. For example, the bishop commissioned pieces from Jonathan Harvey, and he even directed a Harvey opera that the organist conducted. When we went to America for a tour, the Dean came with us. So the Church of England that I signed up to was a church which had three people whom I would see regularly organizing things that I was a little part of, whether it was massive processions from King Arthur's Round Table in Winchester down the high street on Palm Sunday with a brass band and coming into the cathedral nave with thousands of people, or a very kind bishop giving me a strawberry tea at Wolvesey Castle every summer, or the Organist (for Martin Neary was the biggest influence) who was prepared to bare his soul for the music.

I remember a sermon preached by the Dean one St Cecilia's Day. He said, effectively, that the music we had just listened to had more power to communicate the Spirit of God than anything that he could now offer or say. And I remember a rehearsal (for Stravinsky's *Symphony of Psalms*) when the spiritual dimension of our singing was made strikingly explicit: it was not enough to get the music right and sing well; we had to try to convey our own sense of the power of God to everybody through the music. Through these three adults, who seemed to us absolutely rock-solid, we came to see something even larger than the cathedral. The community and activity of the cathedral seemed to point to the community and activity of the wider Church.

I had "given my life to Christ" shortly before I left the Elim church, in the way that you do in that sort of service –

you put your hand up, you go for counselling afterwards and you sign up for bible studies. The expression so often used was "getting yourself right with the Lord". I knew in my heart that He was out there – I have never doubted that, actually, perhaps because I had parents who believed it – but I had put off making any sort of public commitment. Embarrassed to put my hand up or talk about it in front of my parents, it felt to me like something that was private. (I was the sort of little boy who did not want to talk about his school reports, particularly if they were at all critical. I would run away from my father for a whole week if I could, so that he couldn't discuss them with me.) But when I was about to go away to Winchester I must have felt that it was the right time to "get myself right with the Lord". Then, when I arrived at Winchester, I had a sense that through the music something extraordinary was going on. For me that was the defining thing: I'd probably have signed up in any church where the power of the music reached out to me and expressed what I believed about God. It wasn't some feeling that the Church of England was right and Elim was wrong; it was simply that I could sense that what we were doing was Spirit-filled, and it felt absolutely right. Whenever I go back to Winchester Cathedral, all those primordial feelings come back to me, probably because I first heard the voice – really, really heard it – within that building.

Then I won a music scholarship to Eton. It was here that I was required to engage with much more varied perspectives. I remember having a passionate argument with a chaplain who taught me divinity in my first year. The very opposite of a fundamentalist, he brought out the allegorical in his discussion of the Bible stories. Even having been through Winchester Cathedral and divinity lessons in a prep school, I still subscribed to a literal (bordering on fundamentalist) interpretation of the Bible that I had absorbed in Elim, and I got quite upset about being challenged. For me, the change from Elim to Winchester had been chiefly in style of worship rather than in beliefs, which seemed to me not hugely different. At Eton, the encounter with a more critical tradition presented in our divinity lessons meant that I sensed much more of a gulf.

Eton was broadening and good for me. It actually helped me to engage with, rather than to become alienated by, these contrasting traditions and cultures. Above all, I was given unique opportunities to draw them together through music. A distinctive feature of that education was the vast range of optional lectures and talks by visiting speakers. Their sheer diversity, in religious and spiritual terms, provoked a good deal of reflection. I remember hearing Fr Harry Williams and Rabbi Hugo Gryn. I remember being fascinated by several lectures from Hindus and Muslims. One Lent talk in my second term stands out as a key moment in allowing me to explore, and to some extent reconnect, my own diverse experiences. The visiting speaker must have asked the music department for a pianist who could improvise whilst he read from Genesis 1. I remember responding to every line of the Creation story, improvising the music non-stop for ten minutes and being exhilarated by the challenge of trying to depict the visual story through sound. I had seen my father do something like this in Elim when "the Word" was read. (Ten years later, working alongside choir and saxophone, I would lead the improvisation from the piano for a live broadcast on Radio 2 in a vigil for Bosnia, as the then Bishop of Southwark prayed.)

In 1985 I went up to Cambridge, as organ scholar at King's. Here, too, past assumptions were challenged and I faced a new broadening of sympathies and interest. For example, I became aware of the gay issue for the first time (it had not really struck me at Eton, and it would certainly have been spurned by Elim). The college chaplain was gay, and so were some of my new friends. All of this hit me in the first week in Cambridge. I found within that chapel and college a sense of inclusiveness for the first time: King's seemed a place that was unashamedly going to welcome everybody. But the main problem for me at King's (a very personal difficulty for me at the time) was that I picked up a sense, rightly or wrongly, that things were not so much for the glory of God as for the glory of man, and the glory of man meant that it had to be perfect. Nothing could be wrong: everything had to be absolutely in time and in tune and together, and if it wasn't you would know about it the next day because somebody would write in after a radio broadcast and say, "The music from King's today was pretty shocking ..."

The effect of that on me was to make me very, very nervous about making music there, particularly playing the organ. Because I was struggling to meet the exacting demands of playing the organ to perfection, I desperately needed some outlet to be able to express what was in my musical soul. I used to stay up late at night and practise, but the next day I would still be terrified that I would play a wrong note – I had little time to reflect on the fact that I was making the music to help people worship God. It was to do with the whole ethos of the place: Evensong is always perfect there, every day, and it is seen as the best in the world of its type. I know that others singing and playing there were offering their souls completely, but not me – I was too busy worrying about the next note. I had never had that experience before, and it made me lose confidence for quite a while.

So founding Polyphony at the end of my first term was

about regaining control at a time when I felt personally unable to deliver, physically or technically, whereas, through other people in front of me, I could facilitate it. I found that when I conducted I was able to release the sorts of feelings that I had had as a boy. Of course there was an egotistic dimension to it, but it was also about sensing that same power of the Spirit that had previously grabbed me. Standing up there and helping *other people* to make music rekindled in me that "Ascribe unto the Lord" moment from ten years earlier.

Towards the end of my student days as organ scholar, I also discovered a new way forward through improvisation. This healed the nervousness that had confronted me at the start. Having been saturated with a wide range of music, I was able to play in pretty much any style, and one way that I began to express myself was in the liturgy. So I started to improvise and found that I was able to lose myself in the music in a way that had resonance for other people. That restored my confidence.

I hope that my experience at King's made me much more tolerant. Certainly it taught me that there were different ways of approaching things. I learned much from, and began to appreciate, a more liberal approach. Even so, there were odd moments when, listening to a rather academic sermon, I yearned for somebody to stand up in the pulpit and say, "Are you going to give your life to Christ?" There was no longer that direct challenge; it all seemed now to be a musical and aesthetic experience and much more cerebral. On the other hand, simply walking into the cathedral in Winchester or the chapel of King's College Cambridge makes the connection for so many people: it's just bingo!, *credo* – don't tell me any more; I'm convinced. And I think that, had I seen an American evangelical of the type I encountered in Derby in the pulpit in King's College Chapel, he would have seemed out of place in a building that had the music of Byrd and Tallis in its stones. It seemed perfectly right, there, to enjoy a time-warp worship, timeless and traditional. In fact, its time-lessness finally seemed to me the key to its acute reality, to its connectedness and relevance to my own being. There was a sense that others had conducted worship like this through-out the ages and that this, in itself, should be celebrated. So, whereas I had begun to think that you got let off the hook in such a setting because nobody was calling anybody else to attention, on the other hand I came to recognize that one of the strengths of the Church of England is the way in which it embraces very different places, buildings and ways of worship. It has a way of gathering all that has taken place in the past, respecting the link with Christians who have gone before, just as I, by this time, was drawing upon contrasting traditions from my own experience.

By the end of my time in Cambridge I had set my mind on becoming a conductor, but in the meantime I went as Assistant Organist to Southwark Cathedral which, at that time, was a cathedral that did not have a choral *opus dei*, so I had a lot of freedom to develop my freelance work. Southwark was in the liberal tradition and was a fusion of the elements I had experienced elsewhere. There was good liturgy, good music and good preaching – varied and stimulating. For me, there was also the sense that I could offer something to the place, to the space, the whole experience, through sitting at that great Lewis organ.

I particularly remember the ordination of the first women priests in the diocese, for which we had three services over the course of a weekend. The hymn at the offertory was "There is a Redeemer", so the "Thank you, O my Father" was a pretty ecstatic moment for everyone. I kicked the last verse up into a higher key – the sort of thing that we did at Elim, but now more in the style of King's College Cambridge than Radio 2 – and the singing was quite something. I could feel the whole building take off. I saw myself coming full circle and felt a strong link with the days of starting off a chorus as a boy in Derby. There was an overwhelming feeling of being part of the celebration, made all the more powerful by the fact that somebody came to denounce the thing, so that when the bishop asked, "Is it your will that I ordain . . .?" there was a huge eruption from the congregation. But that was in me too, and in the music. As we sang the "Thank you", we declared that something momentous had happened.

So why am I in the Church of England? I want to be part of this richly diverse and inclusive church because it is a church that manages, remarkably, to honour tradition and to explore change at the same time. This is also why I actively seek to influence the Church of England musically. Great music is maintained where traditions are not only valued and passed on but also renewed and re-examined in the light of the diverse experiences and understandings of all those seeking God. It is not just a case of blending old and new: when we are forced to encounter diverse or challenging interpretations, we can actually strengthen, or rediscover, tradition itself. It is this same patterning and interplay – where one tradition comes along and challenges or builds on another – that has been so important in my own development.

For me, the very root of being Christian is inextricably bound up with music. Like Dean Stancliffe, I think that great music speaks more than most words. And I feel that God is honoured while great music is made to his glory. With the music of Bach, for instance, I have a sense of holding sacred pages. It seems to me that there was a laser beam from heaven, straight to his soul. I am profoundly affected by this. When I hear his *B Minor Mass*, I am sorry that I am a sinner: I wish I were not, but I am, and thank goodness there's something that can be done about it. To a rationalist non-believer you certainly couldn't offer that as proof of the existence of God, and you would never convince a King's College Cambridge theologian that God exists because J.S. Bach wrote the *Sanctus* in the *B Minor Mass* but, for those of us who are convinced of it, it offers a robust response and relentless challenge to states of despair.

So now, as a conductor, whenever I work with young people, I am trying to share this tradition of worship and music which I hope they will find as transforming as I have. Moreover, I feel now, more than I have ever done, that the Church's music should be enjoyed beyond the Church itself. Many of my concerts are religious pieces (particularly the Bach *Passions* and the *Messiah*), and I find it exciting that on those occasions an audience of hundreds, if not thousands – many of whom are not part of any church – are actually encountering and exploring a great tradition for themselves. It is vital to present good concerts and other musical events within our cathedrals, churches and sacred spaces, because that brings into the buildings people who wouldn't otherwise be there. And, if the music is led by someone who believes that there is something behind it all, I think that shows. There will be a difference (assuming they are both competent musicians) between the humanist's performance of the *B Minor Mass* and the Christian's performance of it.

In the end, while the style and setting are no longer my preference, everything comes back to the question posed by the American preacher in the Elim church: "Are you going to give your life to Christ?" The Anglican Church can embrace that type of bold directness, while still being able to mediate it in other very different and equally powerful ways.'

9

Alpha Plus

*Former barrister **Nicky Gumbel** had been a curate at Holy Trinity, Brompton (London) for four years when he was invited to take over the leadership of Alpha, the church's introductory course to Christianity. That was in 1990. Within a short time, Nicky realized that the course was proving popular with young people from outside the church – and that their lives were being changed. Since then, Nicky has pioneered the course all over the world and there are now more than 32,000 courses running in homes, churches of all denominations, schools, workplaces and prisons in 154 countries. Nicky is the author of many bestselling books about the Christian faith, including* Alpha – Questions of Life *(the Alpha course in book form). He is married to Pippa and they have three children. In September 2005, he was inducted as Vicar of Holy Trinity, Brompton.*

'I did not have a Christian background. My father was a German Jew, my mother a non-practising Anglican. I was actually born and brought up in the parish of Holy Trinity, Brompton, but rarely went to church as a child.

All my family are lawyers. My father, my mother and both my grandfathers were barristers; my sister is a barrister and so is one of my sons. I myself read Law at Cambridge University, which is where I came to faith: a school-friend of mine, Nicky Lee, said he'd become a Christian and I was horrified. I'd met Christians, but not normal ones, so I was worried about Nicky and his girlfriend Sila and thought I'd better try to bring them to their senses. Because I knew nothing about the Christian faith, I thought I should do some research but all I had in my room was an old school Bible. I blew the dust off it and started to read. I read through Matthew, Mark, Luke, got halfway through John's gospel and fell asleep.

When I woke up, I carried on reading: I read the Bible all that week, and came to the conclusion that what it said was true and that Jesus Christ really was "the way and the truth and the life" (John 14.6). I had a battle going on in my head: shall I just enjoy my life and then convert on my deathbed? But I felt I couldn't do that – it was now or never – so I took a step of faith and became a Christian.

Then it was as if I'd found what I'd been looking for all my life without knowing it. The question, "What is the purpose of life?" had always been at the back of my mind, but at a very peripheral level. Once I'd experienced a relationship with God, it was so obvious to me that this was what life was about that I immediately wanted all my friends to find it obvious as well. I thought that they'd all say, "Oh great, Nicky – thanks so much for telling us." In fact, a lot of them thought I'd simply gone mad, and I probably put many people off. But I did have this overwhelming desire to communicate my experience to other people. Before this point, if you'd asked me what was the worst job in the world, I'd have said being a clergyman in the Church of England. Now it became the thing I wanted to do more than anything else.

My father couldn't imagine anyone being anything other than a barrister. To be a solicitor was barely imaginable and anything else was beyond the pale but, if there was a scale of awfulness, then being a clergyman would have been right off it. It was a deep shock to him and he did not really want to talk about it.

But then he never spoke to me much about anything: the past was all too painful. Until I was 14 and my mother told me, I'd had no idea that my father was either Jewish or German. He had been a barrister in Germany and was disbarred by the Nazis in the 1930s. His father was one of the last people to get out of Germany before the war: he had a friend with a low number in the Nazi party who protected them. That almost backfired, because he protected them for so long that they were nearly too late to leave.

My grandparents left Germany and came to England. Although my grandfather never spoke English, he read it and took *The Times* every day. I didn't know much about them until a couple of years ago when my aunt (who is still alive, in her nineties) produced a box of photographs. It was just like the scene in *Schindler's List*: she went through the photos, pointing out who had died in concentration camps, and so on.

So my father couldn't talk about it and the trouble is, if there is one subject that you can't talk about then every other subject leads back to it, so virtually the only subject we could discuss was the weather. I adored him but we did not talk much about what had happened to me. Since he died, I've discovered from his sister that secretly he was quite proud of my faith. He was 49 when he married, and he died in 1981, a few years after my conversion.

I had actually been baptized as a baby at St Paul's, Knightsbridge, and anyone I knew in Cambridge who went to church went to an Anglican church, so I did the same; all my nurturing was in an Anglican context. When I thought of ordination, it was ordination into the Church of England;

however, although I'd intended to get ordained immediately, it didn't quite work out like that.

When I was 21, I came back to London to do my Bar exams. Sandy Millar had come to be the curate at Holy Trinity, Brompton, and somebody told me that he had also been a barrister. So I asked if I could meet him one day, thinking that this dynamic new curate would be incredibly busy. He opened his completely empty diary, and said, "Yes, today would be fine, or tomorrow, or the next day ..." I think I was the first young person he'd met since arriving.

Sandy started a small group with four or five of us – people he'd known from Durham University, and others. That was how I first got involved at HTB. By that time, I'd started work at the Bar and was completely gripped by it: I was enjoying it so much that I didn't really want to leave. But I reached a point where both my church involvement and my Bar work were expanding so fast that I knew I would have to choose between them. I could have been a Christian barrister, but I wouldn't have had the time to be as involved in the ministry side of things. I realized then that that was my priority. I was recommended for training for ordination and went to theological college in Oxford (Wycliffe). Theological training was an extraordinarily important part of my life. I was fascinated by theology and loved the opportunity to read and reflect on the great theological doctrines and some of the major ethical issues facing our world.

When I was coming to the end of my time at theological college and looking for a curacy, I went to see nine different parishes. None of them worked out, so when I finished my training we moved back to London. That was quite a low point: I'd left the Bar and spent three years training, I was married with three small children, and I couldn't find a job. I was seriously thinking about going back to the Bar (although by then I'd lost three critical years) when Sandy went to see the then Bishop of Kensington who said that I could return to Holy Trinity, Brompton.

So I came back to Holy Trinity and from the moment I started I loved it: I found it all very liberating. My friend Nicky Lee was also working here until 1990, when he went to St Paul's, Onslow Square, and Sandy asked me to take on everything Nicky had been responsible for. That included things like children's church, and I was already looking after the pastors and pastors' training – and then Sandy threw in Alpha.

The Alpha course had been devised by a former curate of HTB, Charles Marnham, as a way of introducing newcomers to the basic principles of the Christian faith in a relaxed and informal way. By the time Sandy asked me to lead it, it was already a regular and important part of the church's ministry. I didn't really want to take it on, but somebody had to. Then, the second time I ran it, I had an extraordinary group of people who came from outside the church and all came to faith; some of them are still leaders in the church here today.

It became apparent that Alpha could be used as a tool for people who were not churchgoers, and that was what really interested me. So we tinkered with the format a bit until it evolved into what it is today. The idea is to give people a chance to discuss the key issues of the Christian faith in a non-threatening way, so each session begins with supper, to give people a chance to get to know each other, and after the main talk we split into small groups to discuss that week's topic. People are encouraged to ask questions, however apparently trivial or threatening, and the course ends with an (optional) weekend away. Mostly it's spread by word of mouth: friends bring friends.

Anyway, the formula seemed to work because it continued to grow, and other churches got interested. People started ringing up and saying, "How do you run Alpha?" And I would spend hours explaining to an Anglican vicar or a Baptist minister from somewhere-or-other how to run an Alpha course, and it dawned on me that I was spending all my time on the phone. So I thought, why don't we get them all together in one place and I'll explain it to everyone who's interested?

A thousand people turned up at that conference (22–23 May 1993) and I thought, "Great, I'll never have to explain it all again!" Then Canon Robert Warren asked us to do a conference in Sheffield, and Roger Simpson in Edinburgh, and after that I thought, "Well, now we really *have* told everybody." Then we were invited to Hong Kong, Zimbabwe, the USA, and so on – and it's been snowballing ever since.

Alpha gave us an extraordinary experience of working with all the different parts of the body of Christ. Other denominations became interested. We started doing conferences for Catholics, the Salvation Army, the Methodists and the Baptists as well as regular ecumenical conferences. Then, travelling the world, we met Lutherans and Episcopalians and Southern Baptists and American Baptists and Russian Orthodox and Romanian Orthodox – the body of Christ around the world, in all its variety and depth.

We loved our time at Westminster Cathedral, when Cardinal Hume invited us there. We loved our time with the Salvation Army, with the Baptists, with the Methodists. We loved the vibrancy of the Pentecostals, and the spirituality of the Orthodox ... We met some remarkable people in China, Russia, India, the Far East and Africa, for instance. It has been inspiring to meet so many Christians, and to see their witness all over the world, and especially in the persecuted Church.

But also, within the wider Anglican Communion, it has been enriching and inspiring to meet with Anglicans of different traditions and different nationalities. Our local church, for instance, has benefited so much over the years from our relationship with Archbishop Henry Orombi and the Anglican Church in Uganda. We greatly enjoyed the friendship which started when he was a student attached to Holy Trinity, Brompton, in the 1970s, and we have watched with admiration as his ministry has grown and flourished in Uganda and around the world.

I think of St Paul's picture in 1 Corinthians 12–14 of the body of Christ, which I'd tended to think of in terms of the local church – some people do this, and others do that, and we all need each other. In fact, of course, it's true of the worldwide Church as well. We can't say, "We don't need you because you're not like us." There's a temptation either to envy or to look down on other parts of the body of Christ but, if we recognize that God has given us different gifts and strengths, together we can create a beautiful body which is attractive to the outside world. On the other hand, if we spend our time fighting each other, that can be very damaging.

Alpha is really about evangelization, but what we began to see at the conferences was that there were secondary spin-offs. Catholics and Pentecostals who might never have come across one another before were sitting side by side, and it helped us all to realize that what unites us is infinitely greater than what divides us. We are sons and daughters of God the Father and therefore we are brothers and sisters. We share a common love for Jesus Christ. We experience the same Holy Spirit. This made us much more aware of the importance of unity, and that disunity is a barrier to evangelization.

One of the strengths of the Anglican Church is its comprehensiveness. It embraces people who by instinct may be either Catholic or Pentecostal – but I'm frequently accused of being Catholic (because of our work with the Roman Catholic Church), or Charismatic, or Evangelical, so I know how unhelpful and divisive labels can be. I'm happy to be all of those things, but I wouldn't want to be limited by any one of them. It's so far from the New Testament, where Jesus made a point of seeking out the individuals behind the labels and the stereotypes. I feel overwhelmingly that I am a Christian, and part of the body of Christ, but within that we have our families, and mine is the Anglican Church. It's been a great blessing and perhaps even the providence of God, that the Alpha movement came out of the Anglican Church, as it may well pose less of a threat to churches of other denominations.

Anglican authority embraces the threefold tradition of Scripture (the *supreme* authority, but not the only one), reason and tradition, both of which are used to interpret Scripture, so there is a balance. At the heart of the Anglican Church is the unchanging message of the Gospel. But Cranmer recognized that, although the message is unchanging, the packaging would have to change "according to the diversities of customs, times and ... manners". We are trying to present the unchanging message in a packaging suitable for this generation, because the big question is how do we communicate to the young people of this country the good news about Jesus with which we as a Church are entrusted?

The age range of those who've taken part in the Alpha course is extraordinarily wide-ranging, but it's had a particular impact on the 18–35-year-olds. That reflects the immense spiritual hunger in that age-group. Demographically, it's the Church upside-down: elsewhere, it's the 18-year-olds who leave.

The Anglican Church is blessed with its buildings, which offer great potential for church-planting and growth; it has also often been blessed in its bishops. Where the institution of the Church embraces the dynamic life of the Church's grassroots and new movements, this makes a powerful combination. It's a bit like marriage: the institution without the love would be unappealing; the love without the institution can be unstable. But where the two are in harmony, it produces a great marriage.

Our own experience at Holy Trinity, Brompton, has been testimony to this. Alpha has had huge support from the Church of England and its hierarchy, both locally and nationally, and we hear increasingly from bishops and theological college principals of the part Alpha has played in bringing people to confirmation and, now, to ordination.

The Anglican Church has always been political, not in the narrow sense of being allied to any particular political party, but in being concerned for the *polis*, the city, the public life of society and the wider community. One great moral issue of our day is that there are hundreds of millions of people dying of poverty, and that should be at the top of our agenda. I feel passionately about the Make Poverty History campaign and getting involved with it, and I think that we as a Church are called to address that sort of issue, both locally and globally. It's such a big issue that it needs the involvement of governments, but the churches can give a lead. We seem to spend quite a lot of time discussing things that don't really affect whether or not people come to church, whereas being seen to tackle big issues like poverty can grab the attention of those who might otherwise see the Church as irrelevant and self-obsessed.

Part of the joy of Alpha is seeing the different denominations working together for the re-evangelization of the country and the transformation of our society. Social action is one area where we can be united on the ground, but I don't think that's enough. We should also be working towards the visible unity of the Church – and the Anglican Church is in a strong position to work with all the other denominations.

I see the Church in this country as a field that has been burned. At one level, it appears dried-up and dead, but if you look more closely there are little green shoots springing up all over the place. Statistics may show a general falling-off in church attendance, but if you look around you see movements, and you find churches that are vibrant and filled with young people who are passionate to change the world. Many people who are not Christians show an openness to the Gospel that I don't think I've experienced previously, and the Anglican Church currently has some remarkably on-fire people in its positions of leadership. It's an exciting time, and I'm glad to be a part of it.'

10

Atheist with Doubts

Ian Hislop *is a satirist, writer and broadcaster. He has been editor of* Private Eye *since 1986 and a team captain on* Have I Got News For You? *since 1990. In 1996 he presented an award-winning documentary series for Channel 4 about the history of the Church of England called* Canterbury Tales. *Recent work includes the Radio 4 series* The Real Patron Saints *and a family history,* Who Do You Think You Are?, *for BBC 2.*

'I've tried atheism and I can't stick at it: I keep having doubts. That probably sums up my position. Edward Norman once said (after he'd grilled me for a bit when I was trying to interview him), "You're in a long tradition of Anglican agnosticism." If I'm a Don't Know, I'm a C of E Don't Know.

My father died when I was 12, which I'm sure had some bearing on my belief. If you're an atheist, death drives you away by proving that it's all pointless; if you're not, it makes you go back and face it – it's one of the rituals that Anglicanism is good at. A.N. Wilson wrote a piece about funerals which suggested that we are all in a long line of worshippers going back about a thousand years, all shuffling slowly to be the next one to fall into the grave, which is a wonderful image. I like a good funeral; I like that a lot.

My father was a civil engineer who was stationed abroad most of the time. I was born in Wales before we moved to Nigeria, and then I went to school in all sorts of places, notably Jeddah, in Saudi Arabia, to a school run by Americans for the children of TWA pilots. We had to salute the flag in the morning, which I liked because I refused to do this and it made me feel more English – ex-pat stuff, really. My father was a Presbyterian Scot and I was baptized as a baby, but without godparents, so there's no one to claim responsibility for my moral welfare, which is probably just as well.

We did go to church, but I don't remember a huge amount of it before I was about 8, after which there was a lot of chapel; unlike most people who had to sit through compulsory school chapel, I was not either bored nor irritated – I always found it quite interesting. I was at an Anglican boarding school (Ardingly College, run by the Woodard Corporation), which was a deeply traditional boys' public school. While I was there, it was suddenly swept by a religious revival.

Two old boys came back – a black guy who'd played football for the First XI, and his mate; they'd joined some Christian organization and they were very, very cool. Christian Union membership went from about 11 to about 300 (which was almost the entire school), and we had a full-blooded, charismatic evangelical revival. Boys who were supposed to be reading the lesson would suddenly start witnessing, American-style, and there were huge prayer meetings for hours after lights out. It was extraordinary, in a closed community, feeling that you were the Early Church, and the staff had no idea what to do about it. Most of them were good Christian men and the headmaster was a former monk, and although they were inclined to think that it was just schoolboy enthusiasm, part of them was paralysed by the terrifying thought that it might be the real thing.

It burned itself out after a couple of terms – during one school holiday, everybody met some girls and gave up completely. To my older eyes, now, it was ludicrous, comic but also incredibly exciting. I've never quite lost that sense of excitement, even though, like an inoculation, it's left me with a certain resistance to that particular evangelical form of religion.

After school I took a year off and went to a kibbutz before going up to Oxford. I was at Magdalen. I went to a Christian Union meeting or two before deciding it wasn't for me; went to chapel very occasionally (there was a lovely choir). Religion was part of the background, but I was not a committed university Christian (of whom there were many). Later, I got married and had my children christened in the college chapel, so that's a place I love.

I went to a confirmation recently in Dorchester Abbey, which is over a thousand years old, and there is that sense that people in this country have been doing this for a very, very long time, and being part of that line of doing is immensely comforting. But English history would have been profoundly different without the Reformation; life without that sort of latitude is unimaginable.

People say, "Why don't we have leadership?" and I tend to feel that if I wanted strong leadership I wouldn't belong to the Church of England. But I like being part of a church where, after the tsunami, the Archbishop says not, "I can see God's hand in this", but rather, "A lot of you might think that this proves it's all rubbish" – and then he goes to the next stage and tells you that his faith is still there, and gives you some reasons why, and some examples, and then you begin to go with him.

101

A Church that allows for science, biblical theology, unbiblical scholarship, changes in knowledge, and trusts its members to form their own opinions and make their own decisions – that seems to me its strength, really. I like it because it isn't inflexible; it has a woolly appeal for those of us with woollier minds. I had a friend who became a priest, whom I admired a lot – I used to do revue with him – but there's also the general Protestant point about no need for personal mediation but each individual having a direct relationship with the Almighty.

I'm often accused of being a cynic, which I'm not, because that implies someone with no belief in anything. I happily admit to being a sceptic, but I think there is a tradition of English satire which is Augustinian in its approach: you do it because you think you are taking the part of the people whom you think are right. So there are no subjects that are off-limits in *Private Eye*, but in the end there has to be at least a moral justification for what you are doing – quite how religious that is is obviously open to question. I certainly don't believe in not speaking ill of the dead simply because they are dead: if you've been rude to people in life then you've earned the right to carry on.

For Christmas 2004 we ran a cover showing the Breughel painting of the Nativity with one of the wise men saying to the shepherds, "Apparently the baby's David Blunkett's", and we had a lot of complaints about blasphemy. But, of the four or five of us in the room when we came up with that cover, four of us must be among the last people in the country who go regularly to church. So far as Anglicanism is concerned, we do a weekly spoof of a parish newsletter which, given the number of people who attend church or read a newsletter, is probably quite a specific parody, not exactly mass-market.

I don't feel that faith precludes humour or vice versa, though it certainly isn't stand-up comedy. But, when I was the age Jesus was when he died, I was one of six 33-year-olds asked to do a Lent talk for Radio 4 entitled *Who Would You Have Been?* and I had an awful, immediate feeling that I would have been one of the smart-arses at the foot of the cross, coming up with bad jokes.

When Channel 4 approached me to do the *Canterbury Tales* series, I suspect their religious remit that year was underdone or something, because it was an unlikely choice for them. It was clear when the project was first mooted what approach they wanted to take – given their audience at the time, it was a case of "Here's some material to be amusingly sneery about", and they thought I would be the person to do it. What turned out was very different: my opinion of the Church of England was not exactly changed, but certainly reinforced by doing a twentieth-century history of it, and I think the series is one of the best things I've ever done.

It was full of marvellous and illuminating stories of immensely good and decent men: despite the ludicrousness and the class problems and the campery and all the things that are easy to laugh at in the Church of England, there remain these beacons of witness which telling that story made me appreciate.

I found when I was making the series that a very early music hall target is the stupid clergyman, and almost from the turn of the century there is a sense of a particular class of decent-ish people trying to do something for another class of people about whom they know very, very little and who don't want anything done for them. There is an inherently ludicrous problem in reaching out to people with this particular message.

I started the series with a bloke called the Ton-Up Vicar, who was a sort of 1960s Father Brown: he wore a leather jacket and had a motorbike and was very keen to have coffee. There is something of that about the Church of England: because it isn't the Catholic Church, and it's not saying "We don't move, we don't change, we don't engage", it opens itself to that sort of mockery. It's also part of what we do in this country: the things we traditionally laugh at are the Bar, the Pulpit, the Throne, so, whatever the character of our national Church, it would have been an object of fun. All the best jokes in Chaucer are religious figures, because of the gap between what is aspired to and the earthly condition; all that's part of the business.

In the Channel 4 series, Malcolm Johnson said, "I see the Church of England as an elderly maiden-aunt. Most of the time you'd like to strangle her, but she comes into her own at Christmas and Easter and she's there when you want her. She's living in a huge house, way beyond her means; sooner or later she's going to have to move out, and she doesn't like talking about anything of interest to most people, like sex or politics" – to which I'd add "or God".

I think even those who like it best note that eccentricity, but it does tip over into affection. There was a story about a bombing raid during the war. Chichester Cathedral had been hit and they found the Dean underneath a table. He'd been there amidst the rubble for hours, and he said, "Don't worry about me – I'm sure there are other people to rescue." But, when they came to get him out, they found him reading *The Odes of Horace*. In any other denomination, it would have been the Bible, or something uplifting.

A great friend of mine, Francis Wheen, is part of a core of very good and funny rationalist writers. He wrote an excellent book about nonsense and mumbo-jumbo, and there's a cartoon of his book launch at which there are all these people and myself and I'm simply presented as "Anomalous God-Botherer", with an arrow. I thought, well I suppose it doesn't really amount to persecution and I'm just going to have to put up with it. But then I suddenly thought, I don't mind – I can't pretend.

There's a quotation from the Psalms that says, roughly, "You gave me life, you brought me up; how can I but worship you?" and of course there's an element of having been born into Anglicanism, or having had it when you were younger, and feeling comfortable and therefore simply going on with it, but the Church of England is about the only Church I can imagine belonging to. There is that bit of the Bible (I'm waiting for someone to say it was a misprint) with the verses about being lukewarm and neither hot nor cold – that's a pretty good description of myself.

I do remember, though, going on holiday with a group of friends and looking round the swimming-pool and thinking, "Well you're reading Danielle Steel and you're reading John Grisham, and I appear to be reading a work by Andrew Wilson about St Paul which I'm really enjoying" – but I do like reading this stuff and I can't leave it alone. I'm interested and I want to know and, even if he's blowing holes in it, I want to know where the holes are.

Another reason for belonging is the need to provide a structure for a felt morality: I feel I'm in a search for meaning and I don't really want to give it up. I don't want to say there isn't any, or I'm going to construct one entirely away from the emotional appeal of the things that I think work, which include music and architecture and poetry, with which we're pretty well endowed and which surround and inspire back.

I like traditional worship patterns and I love church music and all that, so, given the choice, Evensong is for me –

although I still find Sunday evenings very difficult. At about 6.40 I can hear the metaphorical bell going and I think, "That's it: now it's time for Chapel and that's the end of the weekend."

Our local church has a predominantly elderly congregation. I remember reading a review of, I think, *Songs of Praise* in which the reviewer pointed out that everybody in the audience was ugly/dead/crippled/blind, and I thought, "Well, surely that's what it's all about. It wasn't a mission to very attractive young people; if that's what I'm looking for, I can go to a bar."

At moments of crisis, I've met lots of good priests, a couple of whom were women, so I never had a problem with that. Like most Anglicans, I suspect, a brief experience was enough to make me think, "What was that fuss about?"

As far as gay issues are concerned, I can't believe the amount of time that's spent on this one subject: the general public must think that the Anglican Church is only interested in homosexuality. Whether it's African bishops telling you about it in detail, or American bishops talking about same-sex relationships, you would not know that there is any other agenda. Reviewing Malcolm Johnson's quote from ten years ago about the Church of England not wanting to talk about sex makes me wonder if perhaps that's *all* it wants to talk about now, and that's equally worrying.

I've known gay clergy and I remember talking to an old friend of mine who is gay about a church we both knew and of which he'd been a member. He said, "No I gave up that – I don't really want them if they don't want me."

Certainly, making those programmes for Channel 4, I thought how can the Anglican Church be exercised about homosexuality and women when, for almost its entire history, it's been run by homosexuals and attended by women? Heterosexual males are a minority in the Anglican Church. I suppose I'm rather wet on those issues: rather like the debate over women priests (and now women bishops), it may lead to a schism, it may not, but I feel it will end up having to be addressed. Betjeman's biographer marvellously claimed that "He deliberately shackled himself to a dying Church", but I don't think the game's up yet.

I love the quote from Robert Runcie with which I ended *Canterbury Tales*: "The Church of England remains the focus of vague religious expectations on the part of the great majority of the English people" – I can't help saying Amen to that.'

11

Follow Me

Hugh Montefiore *was born into a distinguished Sephardi family in 1920. After Oxford, he served with the army in the Far East during the Second World War before being ordained to a curacy in Newcastle. He spent almost 20 years in Cambridge: as Chaplain, Tutor and then Principal of Westcott House; Dean of Gonville and Caius College and Lecturer in Theology and, finally, as Vicar of Great St Mary's. He became Bishop of Kingston in 1970 and was Bishop of Birmingham from 1978 to 1987. He died in May 2005, the day after his 85th birthday.*

'I was brought up in a Jewish family: not all that kosher, but very devout. I went to boarding school, to Rugby, where, at the age of 16, I had an experience out of the blue. I was sitting in a rather pleasant adolescent gloom in my study when I saw a figure in white whom I immediately recognized as Jesus. I had never read the New Testament, had never been to a service of Christian worship, but I somehow knew that this was Jesus and he said, unmistakably, "Follow me." This is really how it all happened, and it filled me with a very great joy and happiness actually.

But then I was too hot to handle. The nice old gentleman who used to give me Jewish lessons ceased to come, and it was very difficult telling my family (my father was President of the synagogue). The school was scared, I think, of being accused of proselytizing, so they sent me down to the parish church to see the Rector once a week. Eventually he said, "Well, I suppose you'll be baptized in the Church of England", so I said well, yes, I supposed I would be.

If you are converted to Christianity like that, different denominations mean nothing to you. I hadn't the slightest idea what they were all about. I just wanted to be an ordinary Christian, so it seemed to me the thing to do was to join the ordinary Church. My parents – very wisely, I think – said I must wait a year. After that I was baptized and confirmed in the Church of England, so this was how it all began.

I didn't choose Anglicanism because I consciously appreciated its strengths, but I came to appreciate them from the inside. First of all, it gave you room to breathe. I've always been rather an independent-minded chap and I didn't find that I was hindered within Anglicanism for thinking for myself. On the other hand, Anglicanism is apostolic in the sense that it does have the apostolic gospel, and so that tends to keep one on the straight (though not the narrow). Anglicanism is underpinned by the Lambeth Quadrilateral,[1] but it relies on the interplay between Scripture, reason and tradition. Without tradition, you'll think you're wiser than your forefathers; without Scripture, you're rudderless and, if you only base yourself on reason, you waffle.

So I appreciated that: I also liked the C of E's inclusiveness. This may seem rather odd in a bishop, but I'm not a very churchy person. I've done lots of things outside the Church and I think it's very important that one should act as a Christian in the world. I liked being chairman of the Board for Social Responsibility (when there was one). I also became chairman of the Independent

Commission on Transport, and I got involved with nuclear energy. The Church of England encouraged me to do this, and I appreciated its openness. I found that, quite unconsciously, I'd made the right choice.

Something else I came to appreciate about the Church of England is the way in which everybody belongs to it: everyone has rights in the parish church, and anybody can demand to be married there, whether or not they've been baptized. I like that. What Christ did, he did for everyone. I abhor religions that are exclusive, so I regret the increasing tendency towards exclusivism in the Church of England. Some vicars even refuse to baptize – you can instruct people before baptism, but to refuse to baptize is actually contrary to canon law.

I dislike all labels. I refuse to have a label, except to say that I'm C of E. There are strengths about the evangelical movement, and different strengths about the catholics, and there are things from the liberals which I couldn't do without: it's important to have all three. It's a great pity that, because human nature is not fully redeemed, we have this tendency to fracture and to be critical of each other and so augment polarities. On the other hand, the fact that we don't all agree seems to me quite promising really: disagreement, if it's dealt with in a good Christian way, is quite healthy and creative.

I must admit, however, that the present difficulties that the Anglican Communion finds itself in make me want to weep. I don't want to deny others the views they hold – they are perfectly entitled to think that sodomy is an appalling sin (though Jesus actually never said anything about it), but to try to make everybody else agree with them seems to me a denial of what Anglicanism really is at root. As long as we hold the basics of the faith, there should be room for disagreement.

I feel about Anglicanism rather the same as Catullus felt about his mistress: *odi et amo* – I hate and I love. In addition to what I've already said, I love the Church of England's liturgy, which means a very great deal to me. The catholic tradition's use of formal liturgy and language means that the congregation is not dependent on the whims or limitations of the minister. I like the Book of Common Prayer, which has a resonance and a beauty (even though I don't agree with all its theology); I also very much appreciate the language of Common Worship. If you go into an Anglican church today, you may not know which version of the prayer of consecration is being used, but the lectionary and the structure of the service will be the same.

The Church of England was never a church of uniformity but rather of conformity: its adherents conformed to the worship of the Church, but were not required to have a uniform view of doctrine. I inadvertently caused the Doctrine Commission to come into being because, when I was instituted as Vicar of Great St Mary's in Cambridge, I was required to accept the Thirty-Nine Articles. One of them included an acknowledgement that "those things done before the grace of Christ were sinful": my father was a very good man, so this article seemed to me to be monstrous, and I refused to accept it. In the end, I made a supplementary declaration, to say that I was accepting them as true *at the time when they were written*. There was a bit of a fuss about this, so Archbishop Michael Ramsey set up the Doctrine Commission (and made me a member); the first thing we had to deal with was the Thirty-Nine Articles. The present declaration of assent accepts them as our "inspiration and guidance under God in bringing the grace and truth of Christ to this generation and making Him known to those in (y)our care". Grace and guidance are very different from accepting every word as literal truth. They say, for example, that God is reconciled to us, rather than that we are reconciled to God.

Being an established church can be a bit of a burden: it produces an image of the Church which is false to its real nature. The good thing about establishment is that it means we're there for everybody, not just for the club, the elite. Nowadays the privileges of establishment are minimal, but the very fact that we are established gives us a *duty* to criticize the state – to look critically at what the state is doing. Having bishops in the House of Lords may appear anomalous today, but the bishops were the first members of the House when it began and their contribution there is still valued.

The Church has a responsibility to support, if not to lead, and certainly to use its influence for good. We may lack the technical expertise to go into the details of climatology, for example, but we have the moral influence to cause people to take far more seriously the urgency of climate change.

I tried for years to get the Church interested in the environment: at last they seem to be taking it more seriously, but people still don't realize how urgent it is. Take the need to reduce carbon dioxide emissions, for instance. At the moment, carbon dioxide in the atmosphere is 378 parts per million. It's increasing by 2.5 per year, and when it gets to between 400 and 450 we shall have reached the point of no return. In total, 30 per cent of carbon dioxide emission comes from domestic use; industry has done a very great deal to clean up its act, and I wish the Church would encourage much more strenuous intervention in the way we deal with domestic matters.

If we are to reduce carbon dioxide emissions by 60 per cent by 2050 then I believe that nuclear energy is absolutely essential. Wind power is variable, so we will always have to have conventional generators, at least as back-up. As for transport, I wish the government would offer tax remissions for hybrid cars, and also force manufacturers to produce more efficient cars, which they could do. One of the reasons I want nuclear energy is because I'm sure we shall have to go on to hydrogen and, if we are to make hydrogen without causing more pollution, we will need nuclear energy.

Being a member of the Church of England allows (but doesn't require) me to think all of this. It's part of my belief that this is God's world and we have a duty to look after it, so it's imperative for Christians to think about these subjects.

I feel very strongly about accepting homosexuals in the Church. If God made them that way then who are we to tell them that they shouldn't be? Nor do I have any difficulties with accepting homosexuals as priests – some of our finest priests have been homosexuals, though not necessarily practising ones. And I do believe that most lay people are far more broadminded than we give them credit for. On the other hand it isn't helpful to make a big public issue out of it: these things should be dealt with privately and quietly.

There is a real crisis at the moment in the Church of England and the Anglican Communion, but there have been crises before – unsurprisingly, since the Church of England is the ecumenical movement in miniature. I don't believe that the Anglican Communion as a whole matters to the average congregation: they're barely aware that it exists. The diocese of Southwark happens to be twinned with Zimbabwe, just as Birmingham was linked with Malawi, so there are real local links, but the Anglican Communion as a whole doesn't impinge much on parish life. But I believe it is important, because we are part of a universal Church: if we were a single Church on our own, we should feel a little more hesitant about claiming to be members of one holy, catholic and universal Church.

I myself think that the goal of reunion all round is a waste of energy. I can't see that the Church of England will ever willingly say that the Pope is infallible, and I can't see how Roman Catholics can infallibly declare that he's not infallible. So I think that what we really need is to grow closer, to be friendlier and to work together more. My experience of the Focolare movement is that we really do have a spiritual unity when we meet together, despite the fact that we can't fully share in each other's eucharist. That's what I really look forward to: being in full communion with one another, but I don't want to lose the particular characteristics of the individual Churches because they all have their particular excellence. Roman Catholics are very good at sacraments, for instance, and at worshipping with the body as well as with the mind. The Free Churches are often brilliant at preaching, the C of E is really good at pastoral care, and I appreciate that. God forfend that there should be some great process of centralization: the Church of England is already slow enough to make any kind of decision. "Like a mighty tortoise moves the Church of God ..."[2]

It's strange for us in northern Europe, where Christianity is generally in recession, to realize that globally it's booming. People who thought that religion had collapsed are coming to realize that it is a much more powerful force than they'd recognized. That's partly because of the rise of Islam, but don't forget also that it was religion that caused the overthrow of communism. Without the last pope's influence in Poland, I don't think the whole façade would have collapsed. It makes it particularly important that we should communicate better with young people; I don't think we're much good at that. Confirmation is the passing-out parade of the Church of England – they go every week and then you never see them again, except possibly once a year. But quite a lot do come back later.

The divine, by its nature, is something we can never properly conceptualize: it's beyond us. We have to use human words to try to describe God, and we must not imagine that they are final words, because we can never encompass God's majesty and greatness – that to me is very important indeed.

The words I heard when I first became a Christian were "Follow me", and it has always seemed more important to be a disciple of Christ than to be an orthodox believer in Christ. The openness of the Church of England allows for discipleship of all different kinds. I like belonging to a church which contains different kinds of churchmanship, with different traditions of worship, but which focuses its worship on both the Book of Common Prayer and Common Worship. I am happy to worship alongside others who hold views different from my own, for we are all disciples of Christ. I love a Church which is both catholic and reformed, and which is also open to new ways of expressing age-old Christian truth. I love a Church which has pastoral responsibilities not just to its members but to all who live in its parishes. The Church of England is not perfect, and there are aspects of it which infuriate me (and not only me), but, deep down, I dearly love the Church which I joined when I first became a Christian.'

POSTSCRIPT

Hugh Montefiore returned from the war in the Far East resolved to become ordained, and also to marry Elisabeth Paton (whom he had met before the war, at Oxford). The daughter of a prominent Presbyterian minister, she knew from her own childhood experience that she would always share her husband with the Church. She loved,

116

cherished and supported him in all his work, although only his closest friends knew how much he depended on her, not only emotionally and on her traditional nurturing skills but also on her clarity of intellect. Both were delighted when her own gifts were recognized by her appointment to the Liturgical Commission.

When Eliza developed Alzheimer's Disease, Hugh returned her unconditional support in full measure. He retired early to nurture and care for her with great tenderness for many long years, and both Hugh and Eliza in turn received back much they had given to the Church in the loving, unstinting, practical generosity of the parishioners and clergy at their local parish church of St Mary Magdalene, Wandsworth Common. Although Hugh had given his life to the wider Church, it was at the local level that he received much of the social, practical and spiritual support that sustained him in his last years. His parish church was central to his life as an Anglican, and it was here that his funeral was held in May 2005.

Catherine Grace (née Montefiore)

NOTES

1. The Lambeth Quadrilateral is the name given to the four key principles of Anglicanism adopted at the 1888 Lambeth Conference: acceptance of the Holy Scriptures as 'containing all things necessary to salvation'; the Apostles' and Nicene Creeds; the sacraments of Baptism and the Lord's Supper (or Eucharist); and the historic episcopate.
2. Parody of 'Onward Christian Soldiers'. Continues: 'Brothers we are treading / where we've always trod.'

12

Branded a Heretic

*Dr **Rupert Sheldrake** is a biologist and author of many scientific papers and books. He was a Fellow of Clare College, Cambridge, where he was Director of Studies in Cell Biology. He was also a research Fellow of the Royal Society. He is currently a Fellow of the Institute of Noetic Sciences, near San Francisco, and Perrott-Warrick Scholar at Trinity College, Cambridge. His most recent book is* The Sense of Being Stared At, and Other Aspects of the Extended Mind. *He lives with his wife, Jill Purce, and their two sons in Hampstead.*

'I was born and brought up in Nottinghamshire. My parents were Methodists (going back several generations on both sides of the family), but they sent me to an Anglican boarding school – Worksop College, which is a Woodard school, very High Church. So I was exposed to both traditions and I found the Anglican tradition more interesting: I liked the buildings more, I sang in the choir as a chorister and I really liked church music. I come from a family of organists and my grandfather was a formative influence: he was an organist, and I used to sit beside him on the organ stool and turn the pages for him. My father had a broad and tolerant view and was, I think, a slightly reluctant Methodist; he really preferred the Anglican

119

Church and used to go there whenever possible. He loved churches and cathedrals and took me to see most of the English cathedrals when I was a child.

However, by the time I was about 13 or 14, under the influence of my biology teacher (who was also my house-master), I had become very atheistic and antagonistic to religion. He was from a Quaker family, and regarded much of the worship in our chapel as superstition. His basic thrust was that Christianity was no better than all these primitive superstitions that we were so happy to denounce in other cultures, and that the primitive beliefs of savages were in fact far closer to Christian beliefs than most people were prepared to admit. At the time, I thought that was an overwhelming argument against Christianity; I later came to see it as a remarkable strength.

My housemaster was very against religious dogma. He saw science as a liberating force – at that stage in my life I did too, and I still believe that science can be liberating, although it's sadly afflicted with dogmatism at the moment. By the time I was in the sixth form, therefore, I had a pretty standard atheistic, progressive, humanist point of view and, although I had to go to compulsory chapel services, I was the only boy in my year who refused to be confirmed. I saw myself as someone who'd moved beyond religion: science was the future; religion was a thing of the past.

I continued thinking along those lines when I was at Cambridge as an undergraduate, although I always enjoyed Anglican services – even when I was an atheist, I liked going to Choral Evensong in the college chapel. I loved the language, the chanting of the psalms, the anthems – and the service itself did not demand my active participation.

While I was an undergraduate and then a research student at Cambridge, I became increasingly critical of the mechanistic approach to biology. I began to think that this approach to life was much too limited. It left out all the things I found most interesting about animals and plants. The first thing that we did when studying animals and plants was to kill them. So I began to feel increasingly alienated from what I saw as scientific dogmatism and became interested in a more holistic approach. I then became a Research Fellow of my college, Clare, and continued to explore alternatives to the mechanistic theory of life.

When I was 26, I spent a year at the University of Malaya, working on rainforest plants, and on the way there I travelled through India. Going to India in 1968 was an amazing experience which nothing in my education had prepared me for. I spent two months visiting temples and ashrams and gurus, and was very impressed by the richness of the culture, which seemed to have much more going for it than rationalistic atheism, and to be far deeper.

Through some friends, I encountered Hindu meditation and started doing transcendental meditation. The attraction of that was that it didn't require my signing up to any belief system. It simply said: try this and you'll see from your own experience whether it works or not. I found that it did.

In 1974 I took a job in India, working in an agricultural institute. I had enjoyed being in the tropics, and I was not keen to go on doing reductionistic biology in Cambridge. So I got a job working on crop improvement in an international institute in India, and this provided an opportunity for me to explore Indian culture in much greater depth than on my previous visit.

While I was in India, it gradually became clear to me that I was much more Christian than I cared to admit. I found, for example, that my Hindu friends had very little interest in trying to change the world. I was working in an institute that was designed to help poor farmers and my Hindu friends would ask, "Why do you waste your time trying to help these people? It's none of your business; it's their own karma that they're poor and they're suffering." This was so alien to my whole way of thinking that I began to wonder why it was that I had this idea of trying to change the world and trying to help people. Then I realized that this was a secular manifestation of the Christian tradition: it was a kind of progressive humanism, but its roots were in Christianity. Quite surprisingly and rather paradoxically, I found myself being drawn back to a Christian path while I was in India and, as well as meditating, I began praying.

I started going to Evensong at St John's, Secunderabad: I loved the fact that there was a Prayer Book Evensong there in a colonial church in the tropical heat. I was confirmed in the Church of South India by a very old Indian bishop, and for a while I became organist of St George's, Hyderabad, where there was a creaking organ and frequent power-cuts and a man round the back operating a hand-pumping system whenever the power failed.

After I was confirmed, I usually went to the parish Eucharist, and again I liked the fact that there in the heat, with creaking fans in a colonial church built by the Royal Engineers in the 1850s, we would have all the services in Prayer Book English with a Merbecke setting – I was one of the very few English people there. I enjoyed that expression of Anglicanism in its Indian form, but I did feel a contrast between the Christian tradition (which I liked and felt at home in and began to see more and more point in), and the riches of the Indian tradition in which I had become increasingly interested.

I didn't see any way of making a bridge between them, because most Indian Christians had rejected Hinduism. Most Hindus were open to Christianity as a valid religious path, but had rather a superficial knowledge of it. So it was a wonderful moment when a friend told me about Father Bede Griffiths, and I went to visit him in South India. There I found an extraordinary community: a Christian ashram which was extremely Indian, because most Westerners who go to India aren't interested in Christianity and stay clear of anything Christian. So, while Hindu ashrams were overwhelmed with spiritual tourists from the West, the Christian ashrams had few Western visitors.

Father Bede's Christian ashram was very simple, on the banks of a holy river, the Cauvery, in Tamil Nadu. Fr Bede led a very simple life. He wore the orange robes of a Hindu *sannyasin*, and the ashram was a wonderful synthesis of East and West. At the core of it was the Christian liturgy, but we also had yoga and meditation every day. In the services there was Tamil chanting, and we started the morning prayers with a mantra in Sanskrit, so it brought together different traditions.

By then, Father Bede had spent more than 20 years in India and was deeply read in Hindu philosophy. Through him, I found that most of the things I really liked about Hinduism actually also existed in Christianity, but they were hidden or forgotten or submerged. He was the first person to make me aware of the existence of the mystical tradition in Christianity, for example. Another example was pilgrimages: I loved the way that people went to temples, which were sacred places. Then I realized that Europe too had its places of pilgrimage; many had been suppressed at the Reformation, but some (like Walsingham) have since been revived.

I also realized that the medieval churches and cathedrals which I'd always felt a strong attraction to were indeed holy places, many of them on ancient, pre-Christian sacred sites.

Father Bede was an Anglican who had converted to Catholicism and become a Benedictine, and through him I came to know various Roman Catholic contemplatives in South India and also became quite friendly with the Jesuits in Tamil Nadu. So I was in the world of what Catholics call the religious in South India, where I saw an aspect of Christianity that I hadn't really seen before, like the wonderful work done by some of the nuns who (like Mother Teresa) were working with the dying and the destitute, and I visited others who were working with lepers.

I spent about two years altogether at Father Bede's ashram (I wrote my first book there) and it was an extremely happy period in my life. I loved being part of that religious community with its framework of regular services (five a day, following Benedictine rules), and Father Bede's approach enabled me to make a bridge between the Eastern and Western traditions.

When I came back to England after living in India, it was a great joy to rediscover my own religious tradition, especially in the Church of England, which seems to me the natural church of the place. As a result of the Reformation, the sacred places and the integration of culture here are Anglican; the Roman Catholics are a kind of exotic sect, usually in modern buildings in suburbs, which didn't appeal to me at all. I am quite sure that, had I been French or Italian, I would have come back and become a Catholic: As I am English, I became an Anglican – it seemed the natural thing to do.

There is in this country a continuity of sacred place and sacred time, and it's precisely because of that continuity with pre-Christian time that the Church of England in particular is rooted in this land and our seasons and our experience of the cycles of nature. That isn't, of course, the case in the USA, and still less in Australia where Christian missionaries moved in and took over the land, ignoring the sacred places; it's even worse in the southern hemisphere because the seasons are the wrong way round and don't work liturgically.

When I came back, I was living in my home town of Newark-on-Trent in Nottinghamshire, which has a wonderful medieval church with a tradition of daily Morning and Evening Prayer. Going to the weekday services helped me reintegrate the sense of community from the ashram with my life in England.

On Sundays, I usually go to church wherever I am. If I'm staying with friends in the country I'll go to a service in the local village church; if I'm travelling in America, I go mostly to Episcopalian churches, and I find that this sense of connection and local community wherever I go is really helpful. I learned just to appreciate the fact that, wherever I went, there were churches which people took the trouble to maintain and clean and look after, and there were services going on, often with beautiful music.

I found I was pleased that the Church of England was there, and grateful for its existence, rather than feeling frustrated that it wasn't other than it was. I think most people greatly underestimate the richness of the Christian tradition in general and the Anglican tradition in particular – partly because they're not told about it and partly because a lot of people have their minds closed by knee-jerk prejudices, particularly among intellectuals and educated people, who brush aside tradition in an uninformed way.

I do controversial work anyway and, in the scientific world, the very fact that I am a Christian adds to prejudice. The anti-Christian feeling in scientific circles is so strong that anyone who has religious views of any kind is thought to have forfeited any kind of intellectual credibility. I work on psychic phenomena and other unexplained things, and I'm interested in a holistic approach to nature. In fact, I'm interested in a holistic view which integrates things rather than compartmentalizing them, with religion on the one hand and science on the other. I became interested in a holistic approach to science when I was an undergraduate. After my first degree, I spent a year at Harvard doing philosophy, because I had concluded that science was hopelessly limited and I hoped that philosophy might help to provide a wider perspective.

When I went back to Cambridge as a research student, I became part of an eccentric and interesting group of people whose purpose was to explore the area between mystical religion and science, particularly the deeper paradigms or models of reality in science. It was an Anglican–Quaker group that consisted of philosophers of science and scientists and mystics – a monk from the Community of the Resurrection at Kelham was a member of it. Four times a year we lived as a community in a windmill on the Norfolk coast, and every day during those periods we would say the Anglican offices of Matins and Evensong. My main interest was in the scientific and philosophical side; the really exciting thing for me was that here was a group of people, some of them quite eminent professors, who were thinking widely about controversial areas in a way that I found nobody else doing.

Ironically, though I encounter dogmatic attitudes all the time within science, I hardly ever encounter them within the Church of England. I sometimes give talks in our parish church in Hampstead about my research on telepathy with animals and people, or the work of Father Bede in India, for example, and I find people curious and interested and open-minded. I've never had anyone in the Church accuse me of heresy, whereas my experience is that it's easy to be a scientific heretic. I've been proclaimed one on several occasions, notably in a most intemperate editorial in *Nature* which described my first book[1] as "A Book for Burning". The editor subsequently said that I "deserved to be condemned for exactly the same reasons as the Pope condemned Galileo – it's heresy". These kinds of attitudes – the idea that science knows the absolute truth and that there is one single view of nature, which is universal and everyone in the whole world should believe in – in fact resemble the attitudes of the Catholic Church before the Reformation. Science has not yet undergone a kind of reformation and it's still run by the equivalent of colleges of cardinals and is authoritarian and needlessly dogmatic. All of this is in stark contrast to the rhetoric of science, which is about free enquiry and fearless exploration. So for me the Church of England is a wonderful example of pluralism, tolerance, open-minded enquiry and inclusiveness, and I only wish that some of this Anglican spirit would find its way into scientific institutions where it's sadly lacking at the moment.

I would like to see a dialogue, not between science and religion as they are now – institutional science and institutional religion, as currently practised and orthodox – but rather between science and religion as they could be if they both moved beyond some of their dogmatic limitations. If you understand the ecological crisis, for example, as a direct consequence of our sense of alienation and disconnection from nature, then a more holistic approach (like the one taken by Matthew Fox) would examine how a "green" Christian tradition could be grounded in a sense of connection with nature, rather than alienation from it. New bridges between science and spirituality could transform the future.

Father Bede took the view that the Church is like an organism, and I rather agree with him. I see the Catholic Church, not as being the Church of England or the Roman Catholic Church or the Baptists or the Methodists, but as all the Churches, each with a particular contribution to make. Evangelicals specialize in conversion experience: they reach out to people who are searching for a new meaning in life and a fresh path. The Baptists keep alive the idea of an initiation, a rite of passage, much more strongly than any other Christian tradition. Baptism by total immersion is potentially a near-death experience, and my own view is that John the Baptist was a drowner. If you hold people under water for long enough, they are bound to have a near-death experience: they see their life flashing before them, or they experience leaving their body, seeing the light, coming back again and life never being the same – they really do feel they've been born again. All these traditional Christian beliefs make sense if baptism was originally a rite of passage that involved near-death experience.

The Anglican and Roman Catholic and Orthodox churches are good at maintaining the tradition of temple worship, of liturgy, of sacred place and time, and the sacraments, particularly Holy Communion. And the Roman Catholics and Orthodox, and to some extent the Anglicans, maintain the traditions of the religious life and religious communities which again are part of the Christian tradition. The Methodists do very well at maintaining a no-nonsense, down-to-earth approach with a strong reality check: it's all very well in theory but what difference is it going to make to the way you lead your life?

I don't think that any of the churches can do everything, so I actually see the point in a lot of different Christian traditions, but for me the best form of Christianity and the one in which I feel most at home is the Church of England.

Different churches appeal to people at different stages of their lives, and one of the strengths of the Church of England is that it embraces all these different strands. I like the fact that there are evangelicals within the Church of England who reach out to people who don't have regular religious practice. I like the fact that the Church of England includes anyone in the local community who wants to go occasionally to church and to have their children baptized or wants to send them to a church school, or to have a church funeral or wedding, and I like the High Church tradition because I appreciate the liturgy of temple worship.

Obviously all Christian traditions are connected at some level, since they all trace their descent from Jesus and the Early Church, and the Judaeo-Christian tradition. But I think that all religions start from a mystical intuition of a higher consciousness than our own and a source behind the world in which we live, and these are then interpreted in different languages and cultures and traditions.

Father Bede used to compare the different religious traditions – Hinduism, Buddhism, Christianity, etc. – to the fingers of the hand. The palm is the centre from which all come, and they are all different manifestations in human and cultural forms. One of his points about Christianity was that here was the original insight to Jesus and his connection with God, his sense of divine presence in his own right, and his openness to that divine consciousness and the way in which he represented or lived it in human form. But then this mystical, direct experience was packaged in the form of Greek philosophy – the New Testament is written in Greek and carries with it all the cultural connotations of those Greek words, like *logos* (the Word) – and a lot of early Christian theology is heavily influenced by the prevailing Greek philosophy of the eastern Mediterranean.

Then, having been wrapped in Greek philosophy, it became the official religion of the Roman empire and was politically and institutionally packaged in the Roman form, with a hierarchical structure of organization derived from that of an imperial power – a political organization.

So Christianity and its original mystical insights have been packaged in culturally conditioned forms, largely Greek and Roman, and one of Father Bede's missions in India was to see how the original insights of Christianity could be relevant to the Indian cultural tradition. At the moment, Indian Christians have to buy into Western philosophy and Western institutional structures, and very often also into totally unnecessary aspects of Westernism like wearing shoes in church, or wearing trousers and Western clothes – they feel that to be a Christian you've got to be a Westerner.

Father Bede was trying to say that the real roots of Christianity are not Greek philosophy or Roman institutional organization or Western clothing or an alliance with American capitalism – these are historical additions to an original insight.

In the same way, the mystical insights of Sufism are packaged in Islamic clothes and Islamic tradition, Islamic cultural forms; and the insights of the Buddha and of the Hindu sages are in oriental forms. So one can see each of these religions as undergoing historical and evolutionary development, but what lies behind them all is an experience of God, an experience of the divine being, which goes beyond cultural packaging and institutional organization, even liturgical form. All religions point beyond themselves to a source, which is the fount of religious and intuitive experience.

A Hindu teacher I spoke to in an ashram once used a different metaphor but said the same thing. His view was that following a religious path is like digging a well: you're trying to get to the living water that you need to sustain you but, if you're going to reach the water, you have to dig the well in one place – you can't dig a few little holes here and there or you'd never reach it.

I am an Anglican, not only because I am English and born in England and culturally conditioned in that way, but also because I feel this is the right path for me. But I dare say that I had been born in Burma or in Tibet, I would be a Buddhist, and that would be the right path for me. In either case, I would hope that, by following that path, I could sooner or later – perhaps in this life, perhaps in the next – go beyond that particular sort of tradition and cultural conditioning to the consciousness that is the source of life itself.'

NOTE

1. *A New Science of Life: The Hypothesis of Formative Causation* (London: Blond and Briggs, 1981).

13

Converted by St Paul

Fay Weldon was appointed a CBE in 2001 for services to literature. Born in England, raised in New Zealand and taking a degree in economics from St Andrews in Scotland, she is recognized worldwide as one of our finest writers of the fiction of ideas. Her work is translated into many languages. Though now known mostly as a novelist, playwright, short-story writer and cultural journalist, much of her initial work was in television and radio drama, in what she calls the 'great days of the form'. She has four children and lives in Dorset. She became a member of the Church of England in 2000.

'My parents were secular humanists and too ethical to commit me to anything I didn't understand. However, I was sent to a convent for a time as a child, where I was frightened by visions of hell and threats of limbo. Although this was in New Zealand, the nuns came from Ireland and were for the most part elderly and old-fashioned. The patterns of belief that they subscribed to were in today's terms rather extraordinary. I was told I was destined for limbo since I hadn't been christened and was therefore a heathen, and I sat at a desk beneath a picture of St Antony being tormented by devils with pitchforks. Limbo seemed to me worse than hell. I recognized it even then as a description of depression, in which you dwell in a featureless landscape without past or future. One knew, even at the age of 8, that it was a real, solid, all-too-believable place. I asked my mother if I could convert to Catholicism but she said no, and I held this against her for years.

Later, I went to a nice girls' grammar school and sang hymns and loved them (which nobody else there would admit to, but I think they did). My grandmother was musical, a pianist, but the gift bypassed me: I just liked the language of George Herbert and the Victorian poets, the familiar tunes, and the struggle to understand the syntax – which could always in the end be unravelled.

Later on, as an adult (even in my unbelieving past), I would sometimes find myself in a church, for some social event or other – a wedding, funeral, christening – and always found the rituals persuasive, and pleasing to the ear, so long as no one used the Good News Bible with its vocabulary so proudly limited to 1,200 words.

Belief? I like to think I was converted by St Paul. I was asked by publishers Canongate to write one of a series of prefaces to the books of the Bible. I was allocated St Paul's second letter to the Corinthians (Tony Blair had been asked to do it but had turned it down). That meant that I had to read the epistles. I had assumed St Paul was the woman's enemy – better to marry than to burn, and so on — but reading them I found this extraordinary person, this witty visionary, with the most amazing, God-given tale to tell, and I believed him. He achieved the near-impossible. Step by step he turned the untidy rabble of early believers into a unit, which excluded no one, so that it could grow indefinitely. With every letter to this group or that, he sealed belief and principle into an organizational whole. A few pages of crisp thin India paper, 1 and 2 Corinthians, and the world became civilized. "And the greatest of these is Charity."

But I still referred to St Paul in my introduction as a hard person to like, and quoted Ananias, the High Priest of Jerusalem, as saying, "We have found him a pestilential fellow." I knew no better. I had not yet been christened and confirmed. I saw St Paul as more a cunning politician than a man of God. It takes one a long time to shake off intellectual cynicism.

And there was the story of his conversion and how God smote the gaolers, and one always felt very sorry for the gaolers, whose fault it hardly was ... So it was neither just nor kind. I felt, reading, rather as I had as a child: shocked by the way Jesus would blast the fig tree because it was barren. It didn't seem exactly Christian. I'd sung "Gentle Jesus meek and mild" even while the nuns rapped my knuckles for not being able to do long division, and it had stuck.

Time, I thought, to read the Bible. There are bits you skip and bits that fascinate you – like the entire, complex story of Samson and Delilah, there and complete in four short verses (Judges 13–16): think of the paintings, operas, films, literature, that story has spawned. And then there is the Book of Job, and the many commentaries on it.

Let no one talk down the magnificent piece of poetry that is the Book of Job. I was once declared an Islamophobe, by the way, for saying I did not think the Koran was a suitable poem on which to base a contemporary society. To refer to holy books as poetry is just not on in some places, as I found out the hard way. But to my mind the Book of Job is a long narrative poem on a cosmic theme, namely the amorality of God. In the Old Testament, God is the creator, God is power. Job, when he approaches God, stands as the moral force in the world. Faith turns to reproach. Job gives in, in the face of naked power. OK, he says, I'll keep my mouth shut, do what you like – you will anyway. He is immediately rewarded with the most beautiful daughters in all Jerusalem, good health and many fine herds of cattle. But with the New Testament everything changes. You are allowed a glimpse of the person of God, rather than owing a simple obeisance to the principle of omnipotence.

The Old Testament always seems to me a profoundly amoral book, once the firmament has been made. Isaac in particular was not exactly a role hero: walking behind his wives in case he was attacked. One wanted God to choose 'better' people for his favourites. But get to the New Testament, and what a sudden, extraordinary change in the perception of what people are, what we strive to be. The idea of progress from the primitive to the conscience-led was ineluctable. The whole story of the Passion with its emphasis on sacrifice, the sacrifice of your own interest for the sake of somebody else – *Jesus died for us upon the cross* – seems a female inrush into the maleness of the Old Testament. Ask any woman: nothing will ever happen if somebody doesn't give up something. There is only so much to go round. Jesus can't live *and* the souls of the faithful be saved.

I began going to Sunday morning services in St John's, Hampstead (my local church). Philip Buckler was vicar, and he took such a good service that I felt I wanted to join. I didn't like not taking communion – I knew enough not to (I find many don't) – but I couldn't bring myself to say the Creed because I didn't believe it. This was obviously required. Then one day I found I had said it, with a kind of crossing of the fingers, because it's as near as you can get, so I became a member of the Church of England and was confirmed in St Paul's Cathedral, which is an extraordinarily impressive place (I rather disapproved of the ceiling: I thought it was all a bit too voluptuous). Belief, I have found, becomes easier with practice.

I suppose I chose the Anglicans rather than the Methodists, say, because it was the Church I knew, and because its traditions and rituals seem familiar and so bound up with the history of this country. I know the liturgy: knowing it, I can focus my mind on the worship of God. But at the very least just to gather together, once a week, with other people with whom you share experience, to declare a faith, ask for forgiveness and sing some hymns, pray for the sick and be mindful of other people, can be no bad thing.

The modern Church of England makes me uneasy in many ways. I don't like the way it's going in its feverish quest after ratings. I don't like the way individual clergy are given licence, indeed encouraged, in the sermons they write and the prayers they invent, to dominate the service, to the glorification, not of God, but of themselves. Nowadays he/she works in a "team". Why? It would be OK if the teams just stuck to the established liturgy, but they don't. They vie for popularity. My prayer is better than your prayer! A better episode of *EastEnders* ...

I am made nervous by the happy-clappy, the joining together in singing and swaying as in a pop concert. It's mass hypnosis – not appropriate. I am dismayed by the slipping over of services into group therapy, by the determined egalitarianism which seems to favour the tasteless over the tasteful: which reduces the priest to just another "person like us" whose job happens to be that of a parson. He is not: rather a man of God, appointed to be just that, dedicating his life to the task. That's why we give him our respect.

There is a dignity in a one-to-one relationship between you and your Maker which doesn't necessarily involve sharing signs of peace with your neighbour. Signs of peace are fine, but we should do them outside the church, and then we can all go and have a cup of tea.

I left St John's when Philip left because the services changed and everything seemed much more abrasive; then we moved to the country, and now we drive quite a long way to find a Prayer Book service. In too many of our local churches, the older members of the congregation say, "But we liked it as it was." They don't often say it to their bishops, of course, or the new-style clergy: it doesn't seem polite. But they'll say it at literary festivals, should I bring the subject up, and outside the church door once the priest has gone. There is no little dismay in the pews and, should the pews go, much distress. This large swathe of the church congregation, with its wrinkled stockings at the communion rail, belying the call to youth, is increasingly forgotten and neglected, while "youth work" takes centre stage.

There are all kinds of routes to God: you can get there along any number of paths, whether aesthetic (cathedrals and polyphony); soup for the poor (martyrdom); "Who sweeps a room as for thy laws ..." (selfless work) – and they are all valid (although some to me are more valid than others). True, sensing the presence of the Spirit of God can happen unexpectedly in the most ugly church and the most banal of services. But those things don't help.

It's much easier for it to happen if the music is good, or your aesthetic sensibilities are aroused, but even so it's not inevitable. You can sit around being good, or worshipping, and absolutely nothing happens at all, and then it comes upon you unawares – but it's like being asked if you write regular hours or if you wait for inspiration to strike: it's no use inspiration striking you if you're not at your desk.

There's a popular misconception that all religions worship the same God and are all in pursuit of the same thing, namely peace in the world. If only we were! The assumption is that, because we're nice, everybody else will be and, if we think well of other people, why, they will think well of us; and if we don't try to impose our religion on them then they won't try to impose their religion on us. One of the more admirable things about Anglicans is that we are not so sure we are right, but we will still die in the name of faith.

Europe sees itself as a post-Christian society and is setting about making sure that this will soon be the case: there will be a new set of human aesthetics, like human rights, and the old religion will be gone. In the meantime it weakens any faith to teach children that all religions are equal. "Religious Knowledge" as a school subject – in which you study other religions, and take your pick of them as if from a packet of Dolly Mixture – seems to me to be pernicious. As well teach astrology and scientology (perhaps they already do?) ...

Europe wants to lead the world in establishing the first non-Christian, post-nation state. To this end it gently discourages religion, and I suspect, when the authoritarian state turns sour and shows its claws, it will abolish it altogether. They tried it in the Soviet Union. But belief is stubborn. It's hard-wired into us.

Everyone believes in something irrational, be it in the right to choose; seances; that men are the source of all evil (in the West), or women (in the East); the inalienable skill of the acupuncturist down the road; or that the dog-star Sirius is where the aliens live. You may discourage such random and silly beliefs, but you will not abolish them. You can socialize little boys not to rough and tumble and say bang-bang, but it's in their natures and keeps surfacing when you're not looking. People need a legitimate expression for their religious energies: deprived of it, they'll turn fanatical and gullible. Starve Christianity until it closes its churches, or turns them into wine bars, but it's a foolish ambition. The Christian ethos has made Europe what it is

— that and a dollop of Marxism — and it is not so bad. We are governable, malleable and socially conscious; turn your back on it and we may turn (as many do) into Goths and Satanists. "Europe" as a concept is spoken of with religious fervour by its adherents. But I am not sure it will catch on.

Today's under-40s have been brought up in the Age of Therapy: we oldies know what it is to have lived in the Age of Original Sin. Today's theory is that everyone was born good, happy and beautiful, and if we end up none of these things then it's someone else's fault, whether parents', teachers' or spouses'. The concept that we are flawed and in need of forgiveness has become unfashionable. The Pelagian heresy rules.

The word Satan is flung around rather loosely, especially in its adjectival form: satanic forces, satanic enterprises, satanic tax-collectors. But yes, I do think there is such a thing as evil. It descends on a place or a person like a kind of cloud and, to resist it, love alone is not enough. It is very powerful: not like Satan in Job, trotting "hither and thither about the world", but far more intentional. Nor is belief enough: you need something else, not really nameable but it doesn't seem to be "Gentle Jesus, meek and mild", or anything to do with the caring, sharing and compassionate qualities of the female, but rather something comprising those old-fashioned macho qualities of responsibility, integrity, self-will, stubbornness and courage which are traditionally attributed to the male.

Until 30 or 40 years ago, our paternalistic religion promoted a very male model of God, and it was important to allow the *anima* to enter in, because it was being driven out. But now you feel that that side is taking over and we are left with a cosy, warm, fuzzy and extremely female social-worker God: a touchy-feely sensitive kind of bloke ...

I feel vaguely happier with a male priest, just as I feel happier with a male air pilot, but that is probably my generation showing. I'd rather a male priest than a female one performed an exorcism. I feel they'd be better at standing their ground while every instinct cried "Run away". Of course I am not against women priests: it is clearly the vocation of many women. I am not so happy when they see religion as a career path: some do, but then so do some men.

The terror and fear and awe of God is being stripped away and an ordinary gentle Jesus, meek and mild and just like you and me, has taken his place. But awe, not ordinariness, is what brings you to belief. Here we all are on a little lump of stone, hurtling through the universe — what's ordinary about that? How can we endure without faith?

The Church will survive. Something happened at Bethlehem which changed the world, and can't be denied. Yet Christianity in general and the Church of England in particular, is a religion of doubt, of scepticism. "Lord, I believe: help thou my unbelief." That's one of its strengths. But it should not go too far. Unbelievers should not be bishops.

I move mostly among thinking and rational people for whom faith is a real problem. Religion belongs to history, they say, responsible in its time for the wars and atrocities of the past: the future must be religion-free. Remind them that the belief system of the Communists, say, who denied the existence of God, was responsible for countless more millions of deaths in a few short decades, and they do not seem to hear.

If you admit to being a practising Christian, people think you have gone nuts: you have deliberately stepped backwards into the past, where all is superstition and ignorance.

141

Meanwhile, within the Christian community itself, to go to Prayer Book services is seen as another kind of disloyalty – preferring the Church of the past to the Church of the future. Nothing is easy.

People say, "So do you think you're going to go to Heaven?" There is an assumption that you must have joined up for the reward, or because you're frightened of going to Hell. It isn't like that. It doesn't occur to me that, by belonging to the Church of England, I'm better than anyone else and will go there. The gospels are remarkably vague about the nature of Heaven. It does not enter my calculations at all. Indeed, I had a near-death experience once, and the person guarding the gates looked remarkably like Cerberus to me, who stands at the entrance to Hades.

Anglicanism, in its struggle for belief, encourages curiosity, science, technology. Religions of certainty – Islam, communism – in not admitting argument, dampen the spirit of enquiry, which seems to be God-given. When Richard Dawkins furiously denounces religion as a scam and a fraud, disbelief itself begins to sound remarkably like its own belief system. When he talks about inherited particles of religious belief – "memes", as he calls them – he might as well be a believer: there is no clash between religion and science. The fact that one thing is true does not mean that other things are not.

There has to be some division made between the secular and the divine. God's ways are not our ways, but we go on existing, trying to achieve some kind of reconciliation – as in Milton's *Paradise Lost*, justifying the ways of God to man, and man's to God. A noble enterprise. In the Book of Job, you see man used as a plaything, a pawn between the powers of God and the Devil and yet Man is able, oddly, to make them feel bad. That may be why we're here in the first place – to keep God mindful of his duties.

The more Synod tries to accommodate the new, humanist view of things, and the more it obliges young married couples to undertake before God "to be there for each other, to be tender with each other's dreams", and other fatuities, the less impressive, the more banal and the more like everything else religion becomes. The Church is where you wear a wedding-dress, or ask the relatives for the christening. It becomes a "life choice", not something basic at the root of our lives, how we know who and what we are.

Look at the blank, stunned faces of the 'models' you see in the fashion ads: then look at the faces of the church choir, all individuality and intensity of being. The Synod would do better to court tradition, rather than popularity.

Asked to define "Britishness" in a recent political furore, not one of the public mentioned "going to church". Ask a Muslim what being a Muslim means and he'll reply "going to the mosque". There the liturgy does not change, but the belief holds. Our loss of confidence is sad.

The future? Worst-case scenario: the Book of Common Prayer will be banned, and most of the familiar hymns also, for improper sentiments. ("We plough the field and scatter" will become "We diversify and beautify, within quotas we're allowed".) The licence for a church choir will become so expensive that all singing will be karaoke-style, contents overseen by Sir Bob Geldof. The clergy will then depart *en masse* for the social services where they are better paid, decently housed and can do much the same thing as before. Churches will close. No one will protest, because those who choose to can enjoy computerized services in the safety and comfort of their own homes, with a virtual and hygienic wafer and wine, by interactive DVD. Worse, the whole nation swings to Islam, where it finds continuity, rules of conduct, formality and majesty.

Best case: we go on as before, arguing and bickering, and the congregations creep back – down the road at the Christian Centre they have noisy, lively, cheerful, young congregations of two to three hundred on a Sunday morning – and I am completely wrong to doubt or worry.'

14

Signposts in Society

Lucy Winkett was born in Wiltshire and, after studying history, living in a L'Arche community and training as a soprano, went to Birmingham to study theology. She served her title in east London, became Chaplain at St Paul's in 1997 and is now Canon Precentor, with responsibility for music and liturgy.

Instinctively, my answer to the surprisingly challenging question 'Why are you still an Anglican?' is something similar to the motif of a recent innovative film. Being an Anglican is like *Being John Malkovich* (if you are John Malkovich, that is), which is to say that I was born an Anglican and it is an integral part of my identity. It influences the way I understand the world. I wear Anglican spectacles to look at life, and to take them off would mean not being able to see. But it is not, now, just unthinking instinct: over the years, I have discovered I am Anglican not just by birth but by conviction. I have found myself converted to Anglicanism from the inside.

There is much to amuse, infuriate and irritate about Anglicanism, and its constituent parts are, to paraphrase St Paul, as different from each other as an eye from an elbow. Does it matter that, as we recite our mantra of unity in diversity, it is not always clear what the Anglican

145

Communion is? It looks like a collection of institutions, each with its own culture, codes and jargon. The Church of England's caricatures are now well established in the UK, with the media, as always, telling us about ourselves in the stories of Dibley, Walford, Emmerdale and Ambridge. But being an Anglican is not about being part of an institution so much as being part of the *ecclesia*, the body summoned forth from humanity, marked by the life of Jesus Christ; the body which is named, called and led into the future by a crucified and risen Redeemer.[1]

I speak from the perspective of cathedral ministry, a privileged and invigorating context from which to reflect on Anglican identity. Cathedrals embody a paradox: they function close to the centre of the Established Church (although not perhaps at its heart), yet they are also refreshingly secular places in which to minister. Large numbers of people visit St Paul's Cathedral, for example, and a high proportion of those do not come for any identifiably religious reason. They might come because it's on their list as they 'do' London, or because their mother spoke of seeing the dome survive the Blitz. They come because Diana was married here, or because they'd like to compare it with St Peter's (where they were two days ago). They come because they think it's a Roman Catholic Church and they want to attend the midday mass, or because they think it's St Paul's underground station.

However they come, when they arrive, they all look up. The walls of a cathedral enclose a large public sacred space into which men, women and children wander for as many different reasons as there are visitors. Cathedrals speak of the 'otherness' of God, at the same time as being intimately embedded in the society they serve. And that's Anglican.

If we start to believe we are a separate (religious) institution that exists alongside other institutions, then we are simply another way for people to fill their leisure time. Governments may consult us because we're part of the voluntary sector, and tourist brochures trumpet the heritage of Anglican churches and cathedrals as something to see, but our self-understanding has to be clearer than that. We are not a separate society, or state, or organization. The Anglican Church doesn't exist as a result of a set of decisions, or a series of meetings, or a strategy. These managerial tools are useful but not ultimately defining of our character or purpose. The Anglican Church happens wherever Anglicans pray together through the complexities and subtleties of life in the world, expecting to find God there, waiting to be discovered.

Cathedral ministry is a distinctive part of this wider Anglican identity. Cathedrals are a presence in society, hosting, waiting, talking, listening to the rhythm of the city around them; they flourish on the boundary of sacred and secular. To borrow a geological metaphor, cathedrals are built on society's fault-lines and when the tectonic plates of, for example, church mores and business culture clash, we have to learn to withstand the shaking of the foundations that sometimes follows. These broad movements – shifts in culture, economics, patterns of association or behaviour – can throw cathedrals into confusion and cause us to ask fundamental questions. What are we for? What is the relationship between heritage and mission, commercial activity and prayer? What are the ethics of tourism? Is it enough to be a church which allows continued anonymity in its worshippers and carries a memory of faith vicariously for those who never come?

For example, it's often said that one of the precious gifts that the Anglican Church offers in the context of British society is Choral Evensong. Cranmer's Prayer Book emphasis on the Incarnation, together with the transcendent sound of choristers in an evocative acoustic, is a compelling combination for an exhausted urban population looking for peace. The conversational rhythm of the versicles and responses, the ancient wisdom of the psalms, the prophetic energy of the *Magnificat* and the sure touch of Simeon's *Nunc Dimittis* faith, together with anthems that may be from before the Norman Conquest or written especially for that service – all of these elements create a sacred space, infused with music, within which can be held that day's disappointments, delights and disasters.

As we try to explore the future of this tradition of faith, we find that it is part of the cultural life, not only of cathedrals but of the Church in general, and is umbilically attached to the cultural life of the United Kingdom and beyond. What we are saying, as we sing Evensong each day, is that all our life is prayer and, towards the end of each cycle of sunrise/sunset, we invite any who find themselves in the street by a church to come in and rest. They will not be asked to do anything; nothing will be demanded of them except that they respect the rhythm of the liturgy as we offer, day after day, the life of the world to God.

From this confident Anglican base, we can explore music and liturgy with a spirit of cultural curiosity. There is no time or place or style that is necessarily outside the scope of 'cathedral music'. We are guilty sometimes of muddling taste with standard: we talk about 'modern music' when what we actually mean is The Carpenters. Being able to read ourselves culturally is something that Anglicans should be good at, because we are embedded in that wider society. To echo John Donne, Anglicans should never try to live on a cultural island. We are part of a worldwide Communion and we have a chequered history. We should remember, among many other things, that in the eighteenth century slaves were transported from Africa in *The Good Ship Jesus*. In a British city where I can order a pizza which is delivered by a Sikh, where I can hear a hundred languages on a busy Saturday afternoon, and in a communion where the largest number of Anglicans are black and female, monochrome liturgy is unacceptable. Like those seeking a memorial to the genius of Sir Christopher Wren, we too should 'look around us' and see what is there.

Music is performed live in cathedral worship and we will struggle with the expectations of a public educated in recorded and downloaded music. Music here is not perfect, mistakes are not airbrushed out: you can see (and be distracted or inspired by) those making the music. The worshipper cannot control the volume or the content. It is given, and it is offered as a gift. Once you have chosen to come, all you have to do is stay.

The fact that real people are singing and playing affirms the importance of another principle dear to an Anglican heart: that of presence. To continue to gather – literally to meet each other face to face – is both a spiritual discipline and an act of resistance in a world that withdraws regularly to its laptop to express its isolation in cyberspace. I've been interested and invigorated by experiments such as the Virtual Church; when I preached online, the experience of the presence of other people was one I found surprisingly moving and real. But there is still the principle of encounter, exchange and instinctive physical behaviour which remain vital and enlivening parts of our collective worship. Cathedrals, with their tradition and resources, can contribute enormously to the affirmation of the principle that it is still important to be present in body, as well as in mind or spirit.

Bodies themselves are a little thin on the ground sometimes. At a poorly attended cathedral office, I'm conscious that we probably look like an ecclesiastical branch of the Sealed Knot, re-enacting events from the seventeenth century in historical clothing for our own enjoyment. Anglicans are often accused of self-obsession, but we are easily amused by our own foibles and perhaps that's the best sort of navel-gazing.

It is said that you can tell which denomination of church building you are in by going into the vestry. In a Methodist vestry, you will find a picture of Jesus the Good Shepherd; in a Roman Catholic vestry, you will find an image of the Sacred Heart of Jesus. What you will find on the wall in an Anglican vestry is a full-length mirror. We can suffer from ecclesiastical sartorial anxiety and sometimes that translates into hierarchical giddiness. Just as predictable as some clergy rushing to the back of a procession are the phone calls from any number of clergy before a large cathedral service: 'What shall I wear?'; 'Where shall I sit?'; 'I hope you're not going to give me that old tat you gave me last time.'

We Anglicans like order, particularly in worship, and our liturgy shapes our doctrines and beliefs, but liturgical perfectionism can become a sterile coping mechanism which reassures us we are doing something well when we're too afraid that we're failing. I am certain we can have more confidence in ourselves than that, and place our trust, not in numbers, but in the embodiment of just and right relationships with God and with each other, which is what good liturgy can be.

The fact that many visitors do not think of themselves as churchgoers, even after they've been to St Paul's, doesn't trouble me too much, nor does it dull my sense of being involved in primary mission. I believe in transformation – indeed transfiguration – as a pattern of Christian life. But that can happen over a long period of time: the encounter any one person has with a church community, or a priest, or a Christian with whom they work, will make but a contribution to the whole. It isn't that Anglicans have low expectations: we have high hopes as we constantly try to be signposts in society to the reality of God beyond us. But we are pragmatic, and ordinary, too, in our acceptance that God takes the stuff of our lives – even such pedestrian things as bread and wine – and transfigures them into the means of salvation. We are there, as William Temple told us, for the people who don't belong. We are there when people get sick, fall in love, find life confusing or lose their way. We are simply there. This might (as the old joke goes) explain why most people in Britain are as reticent about churchgoing as they are about their visits to the bathroom. You don't say that's where you're going, you don't talk about it when you come back – and you certainly don't discuss what happened when you were there.

Being an Anglican these days is a bit nerve-wracking. There's so much to be cross about as our internal rows continue. We move in tone from diplomatic to furious, anxious to mocking, pleading to bullying. It's dispiriting when the tone of our debates becomes shrill and we indulge in what the novelist Sara Maitland calls 'competitive vulnerability' ('I'm more hurt than you are'). But at least we are talking about it.

I have never accepted the quip that the Church is 'being dragged into the twentieth century' at the beginning of the twenty-first. Yes, we were late off the mark in recognizing that women had souls, and it's taken us fourteen hundred years to recover from that confusion. But, at the beginning of this third Christian millennium, the Anglican Church is addressing issues that might seem to have been resolved in British society at large, but actually haven't.

Legislation helps to enforce justice but, in discussions

151

about human identity and society, it's hearts and minds that need transformation. It is still rare to see a woman drink alone in a pub, or a man running a nursery. From yobs to ladettes, to the recently reported death of 'Superwoman', our understanding of gender and sexuality is in flux; the roles of men and women and the nature and definition of family are not settled. All these strands take us in new directions as we understand more and more about who we are. The Anglican Church has a vital role to play in the shaping of society in the light of scientific questions, ethical dilemmas, cultural expectations and the Christian gospel of liberation. The opportunities for peaceful cross-cultural exploration and interaction are unique in these islands and, where gender is concerned, the Church could help the residents of Mars and Venus visit, and listen, and walk in each others' shoes for a while.

It really isn't easy being a woman and a priest in the Church of England. Well, it's easier if you are content to breeze through with your eyes and ears shut; but to acknowledge the assumptions and recognize the patriarchy with which the institutional Church is still enamoured is to see the emotional scaffolding that keeps men and women afraid of a greater prize – freedom to be ourselves.

Walking down the street in a dog collar is, despite Dawn French, still unusual enough to elicit comment, or at least a bit of staring. Whether or not this is fun depends on what day it is. Even in church, it seems that it can be disorientating. One day a visitor was standing under the dome in St Paul's as I presided at the Eucharist from the high altar, so he could hear but not quite see me. When one of the vergers asked if he needed any help, he simply asked in genuine bewilderment, 'Why is that priest speaking in a woman's voice?'

Being an Anglican ordained woman is all at once marvellous, profoundly fulfilling and incredibly frustrating. Ten years after being ordained, I can still veer easily, in gatherings of clergy, from being sure-footed to wrong-footed to cack-handed. It reminds me of Ginger Rogers, who memorably said, 'I did everything that Fred Astaire did, but backwards and in high heels.'

It means wanting to answer the question that your presence seems to raise, but not quite being able to do so. Vestries are still locker-rooms from time to time, and groups of men together – straight or gay – will exclude out of nervousness, or well-meant attempts to give women a special place. Sometimes, in the middle of a discussion about some corner of the church's activity, you'll realize that you're 'them' when you had thought you were 'us'. Ordained women, by our nature, can never be chaplains to the status quo. The presence of women, alongside men, representing Christ at the altar and the people before God has brought a liberating theological and liturgical gift to the Anglican Church. We need to explore together how this can better express the extraordinary truth that God is with us.

All of us, clergy or lay, male or female, need to know too about the shadow side of Christian ministry: our various martyr complexes, saviour fantasies, victim mentalities and tendencies to pastoral lust and, more seriously, the dipping morale that really does seem to dip very low among clergy sometimes. If we can find a way to take God more seriously and ourselves less so, we will soften our defensive and worthy tones, and perhaps generate more light than heat in our debates.

Anglicans can find a way to do this, especially if we are not afraid of the media. Because we are woven into the fabric of this nation, our conversations, arguments and mistakes are public and obvious. We end up washing all our linen, dirty or not, in public. Anglican arguments (in the sixteenth century about authority, along the way about our ritual practice and now about human identity) are following a parallel path to the Enlightenment/post-Enlightenment/Darwinian/post-Freud agenda of the society in which we are embedded. It seems to me that this is a sign not of our weakness but of our relevance and integrity.

I am angry when I see the bitterness that sometimes erupts, and I feel restless for change in terms of our consecration of women bishops, our taking seriously the ethnic diversity of our Church and society, and our continued inability to celebrate diverse sexuality, to name but three current issues. But, as an Anglican, I am enthusiastic about a debate that wrestles with Scripture as a word that is studied, preached and spoken, rather than simply written, because I love the Bible, not primarily as a collection of printed books, but as a soundscape spoken, sung, laughed and cried over down the centuries. I have learned so much from an Anglican treatment of Scripture that recognizes context as important: not only the context of the author, but the context of the reader within the God-breathed freedom of the Spirit as interpreter.

For Anglicans, scriptural truth isn't so visible as a sentence we can copy down, nor can it be simply the Ephesians sword of steel with which we run one another through. Scriptural truth is sculpted before us in the voices of the prophets, the psalmists, the evangelists and the apostles. Scripture, for Anglicans, can't be a 'captured' word, written on a page (although we do like to have a book to hold), but a free and living word, quickening Church and society.

Being Anglican is learning to forge meaningful relation-ships on an anvil of profound disagreement. Dare we believe that Anglicans can be alchemists, unafraid to be open to one other in the belief that something precious and new can be created in the furnace of disagreement? Surely the unity of the holy, catholic and apostolic Church is ahead of us, rather than behind us, and – to disagree with the seventeenth-century Archbishop Laud – the unity we seek can't be hewn from uniformity.

We are too quick to turn our Anglican ploughshares of scripture, reason and tradition into the swords of ejection and aggression. It is unAnglican to do so. This has nothing to do with being nice, and it has nothing whatsoever to do with manners. It is the difference between being peace-lovers and peace-makers. Making a just peace is demanding, energizing work, and at times will cost us everything. To quote Dean Inge (a former dean of the cathedral where I now serve): 'Don't imagine you're thinking when you are simply rearranging your prejudices.'

But, in the end, the politics of the institutional Church is not where Anglicanism lives and breathes. I am an Anglican because I'm proud that women and men are baptising, marrying, burying our people – the people who live in our patch. I love the Anglican Church: its diversity, its roominess, its capacity to hold me and all my muddle. I love its poetry and theology, its commissioning of the arts and its self-deprecating humour. I love its involvement in politics and the issues of the day, both local and national. I love the fact that every soul in these islands, whoever they are, has someone to pray for them. Being Anglican is being at home: the place within which I can challenge and argue, the place from which it is safe to travel, and the place to which I guess I will always, eventually, return.

NOTE

1. I have been influenced here by the theologian Nicholas Lash in *Holiness, Speech and Silence* (Aldershot: Ashgate, 2004).

15

Home Thoughts from Abroad

Edward Lucas was born in 1962 and educated at Winchester, the LSE and the Jageiellonian University, Cracow. He has been a foreign correspondent in Eastern Europe since 1988 (chiefly in Moscow, Berlin and the Baltic states) and is currently Central and Eastern Europe correspondent for The Economist. *He is married to the Roman Catholic writer and broadcaster Cristina Odone and has three children.*

St Saviour's Anglican church is built of brick, and it stands on British soil. But it is hundreds of miles from Britain, in the Latvian capital, Riga: the earth below its foundations was brought there by patriotic English merchants in the nineteenth century. St Andrew's has similar Victorian church architecture – but it's in Moscow. In my nearly twenty years as a foreign correspondent in Eastern Europe, these and other Anglican churches of the European continent have provided the spiritual landscape for my life, and my education in Anglicanism.

I thought I knew the Church well. I was brought up in an Anglican family, studied religion and worked as a journalist for the BBC's religious affairs department. There were, I reckoned, at least seven kinds of Anglican. My crude caricatures went like this:

1. *The evangelical* – well-scrubbed, austerely dressed; the self-conscious, even smug, heir to the traditions of the Reformation and, before that, the Early Church. He worries that many Anglicans are Christians in name only, but likes the idea of evangelizing them. He sees the Church, not as the bride of Christ on earth, but as the 'best boat to fish from'.

2. *The Anglo-Catholic* – scented rather than scrubbed, and elaborately coutured. Would be a Catholic in Italy, or Orthodox in Greece. Liberal-minded on the Bible; nit-pickingly precise on details of liturgy and vestments. Loves the Church; less keen on outsiders. Worries that other Anglicans do not have the right idea about sacraments and neglect saints' days.

3. *The liberal* – relaxed in dress and manners; open-minded to a fault; sees central tenets of the faith as dearly held but hard-to-believe, valuable in a symbolic rather than literal context. Finds evangelizing distasteful and worries that other Anglicans make the Church look offputting.

4. *The traditionalist* – British to his bones; sees, often unthinkingly, the Church of England as part of the national identity, the wellspring of the country's literary and constitutional tradition. Loves the Book of Common Prayer and the King James version of the Bible. Dislikes modern Britain. Thinks other Anglicans are faddy and overexcitable.

5. *The radical do-gooder* – goes to church because he wants to bring down the mighty from their seats and exalt the humble and meek; to dump the debt and save the rainforest. Right-on politics usually combined with ultra-liberal theology. Regards other Anglicans as stuck-in-the mud and introverted.

6. *The community-minded* – a staunch supporter of the playgroup, the choir and the youth club; admires the vicar more for his people-skills than his preaching. Hazy on doctrine; thinks other Anglicans are rather 'churchy' and intense.

7. *The loyalist* – faith rests on shaky foundations, but unwilling to ditch the Church altogether (at least while his parents are still alive). Feels that an hour a week of reflection and hymn-singing makes him a better person. Finds other Anglicans too clubby.

These caricatures (admittedly crude) were all features of my life. It didn't put me off churchgoing altogether, but it did strike me as an odd feature of Anglican Christianity that each strand of the Church attracts vehement criticism from other parts of the Church. The evangelicals in particular seemed to regard all other motivations for churchgoing as peripheral: you're either saved or you're not. If you want a social club, a political party, or a family get-together, go to one.

Other bits of the Church were equally (un)charitable, regarding the evangelicals as simplistic and narrow-minded. Many outside Anglo-Catholicism regarded that as something of an affectation: a club for people who like prancing about in strange costumes amid clouds of incense, pretending to be holy. Those bits of the Church that believed in the virgin birth, the physical resurrection and the ascension were uncomfortable with those that didn't. The radical do-gooders distrusted the traditionalists, and vice versa.

It was tempting to conclude from this that Anglicanism was a ragbag of warring and contradictory beliefs, a historical accident now facing a deserved and inglorious demise. In a world which likes clear boundaries – gay or straight, pro-Bush or anti-, vegan or not – the ambiguities of Anglicanism seemed quite out of place.

But, even before I went abroad in the mid-1980s, I began to see that this argument could be turned on its head. If you agree that it is rash to be too certain about the future of Christianity then a dose of inclusivity and tolerance is wise. Take three examples: first, if women priests and bishops prove to be a temporary enthusiasm, destined to wither away, then the traditionalists will be vindicated and recover their central role. If, on the other hand, there is an overwhelming and permanent shift going on in human understanding of women's roles, then much of Anglicanism has already grasped it.

Secondly, if there is a general revolt against literal readings of holy texts then Anglicanism offers a ready framework for a Christianity that does not treat the Bible as a history-book-cum-instruction-manual. If instead there is a renewed interest in devotional use of Scripture, Anglicanism has a powerful intellectual tradition to support that, too.

Thirdly, the sacramental tradition may perhaps prove to be a hangover from a premodern age, and will die out along with indulgences, relics, exorcisms and prostrations. Or maybe sacraments will prove to be the key to religion in a postmodern age, where people seek symbolic expressions of hidden meanings. Either way, Anglicanism can accommodate the shift in spiritual appetite.

I appreciate this breadth all the more because my own Anglican faith has veered so sharply between all points of the ecclesiological compass. I grew up in a family where churchgoing was an unquestioned part of life. My father, a philosophy don, advised the Church on doctrine; my mother has a theology degree. As a teenager, I was an evangelical; as a student, a right-on modernist, combining ultra-liberal theology and ultra-liberal politics. As a busy young journalist, I found my faith stretched and resorted to habit and tradition, joining the Prayer Book Society and going to church mainly to sing hymns and make good resolutions.

It was only when I was travelling abroad that I began to feel at ease with the Church. As a student in Cracow in 1986 (with no Anglican church nearer than Berlin), I sought out the tiny Methodist congregation, and tingled to the sound of familiar hymns sung in Polish ('Abide with me' was a local favourite). It was an experience that both prompted homesickness and cured it.

Working as a Western journalist in Eastern Europe before the collapse of Communism was a lonely, sometimes scary experience. The outside world was largely uninterested – the Berlin Wall seemed a permanent fixture – and friends and colleagues were thin on the ground. Every contact with a local brought an ethical dilemma. Was the nice girl I met at a lecture in East Berlin truly a secret dissident eager to pass information to a friend from the free world, or a Stasi plant trying to embarrass me (and, worse, the BBC)?

As I wrestled, in my callow way, with these problems, I found the Anglican congregations in West Berlin and, later, Prague, Riga, Vienna and Moscow, became a central part of my life. There were big contrasts: the Berlin services were in a splendidly fitted-out military chapel; the Prague ones, until the collapse of communism, were celebrated in the basement recreation room at the British embassy by a visiting priest from Vienna. But for me the effect was always the same – and ever stronger.

Of course there were plenty of services in local languages, and I attended them when there was no alternative. But I found nothing to match the pull of a familiar liturgy, of fellowship with like-minded believers, and those beloved hymns. The effect on the soul was similar to that of Marmite on the tastebuds. Admittedly, analogies like that make expat congregations easy to caricature. People who would never darken a church's doors in England start coming, because they are bored and lonely. There is a sometimes ridiculously self-conscious Englishness, not always confined to the English members of the congregation: I remember, after one service in Berlin, hearing an elderly German woman hissing reproachfully to the (also German) intercessor, 'You forgot to pray for our Queen.'

But behind the absurdities are huge pluses. An Anglican church abroad can play a role which is muffled at home. In Eastern Europe, it represents the triumph of good over evil. St Saviour's in Riga was closed by the Soviets in 1940 and turned into a youth club. St Andrew's in Moscow was confiscated by the Bolsheviks after the Russian Revolution, and clumsily converted into a recording studio. Even then, the architecture was a mute witness to happier days, and local Anglophile believers would offer a silent cheer as they passed. But regaining and reconsecrating the buildings after the collapse of communism was a symbolic triumph: atheistic, xenophobic intolerance was vanquished, and a precious historical and spiritual feature of both cities was restored to its rightful use.

In communist Czechoslovakia, where atheism was the state ideology and the church leadership had to a large extent been bullied and suborned into making shameful compromises with the system, the existence of a 'real' Church, however tiny, was of symbolic importance. And, peripheral as the Anglican services were, they made me feel that I was doing something in my spiritual life to stand alongside the underground priests and dissident pastors whom I met in my journalistic life.

In Berlin, the Anglican Church also had symbolic value.

One strand, as in Prague, was fighting the good fight of the Cold War. Many members of the congregation were officials (actually spies) and soldiers from what was then the huge British official presence in Berlin. They were clever, brave and friendly – and I found the atmosphere in the congregation a refreshing contrast to the ignorant peace-nikery of much of the Church back home. Another, contrasting but complementary, element of the congregation was reconciliation between old foes. The congregation also included elderly couples consisting of British servicemen who had been posted to Berlin (in the days when part of the job was to keep a vanquished enemy subdued), and local girls they had met and married.

In the new conditions of freedom, the Church remained a protagonist, but this time in another culture war: between the spiritual values of Western civilization, and the brash, avaricious ways of post-communist capitalism. The end of totalitarianism left a moral vacuum, where greed was elevated to a virtue, and brutality overlooked. Many expatriates found the temptations overwhelming: compared to life in respectable Western countries, the money was far better and the fleshpots far fleshier. One (bachelor) journalistic colleague of mine in Moscow confided that, in his first six months in town, he had never gone to bed alone or sober. For Westerners living and working in a city where swindling, promiscuity, drugs and drinking were everyday pursuits, church was a place that refreshed and inspired.

For me, there was an increasingly important extra dimension. My marriage was breaking up. There was a danger that my children would end up living far away, and my contact with them would be sharply limited. As my home life deteriorated (and my children were no longer able to come to church), St Andrew's in Moscow kept me from disaster. The shabby, desecrated church fabric, like the wounded body of Christ, matched my own feelings of hurt and despair. Weeks would go by when it was only at services – sometimes the Sunday Eucharist, sometimes the daily said evening prayer – that I felt (rightly as it turned out) that hope of a happy future was not altogether lost.

The miserable physical state of St Andrew's highlighted another powerful way in which a church abroad inspires commitment: through its vulnerability. For most congregations in Britain, the parish seems a permanent fixture. Even if it closes, or is merged in a team ministry, life will go on. For an expatriate congregation, existence is much more precarious. St Saviour's and St Andrew's are both in advanced states of disrepair – St Andrew's in particular needs millions of pounds to keep the rain out and the roof on. Everything portable was stolen or destroyed under communism, and the interiors disfigured by hideous, Soviet-era conversions. Obtaining even the simplest church furniture requires head-scratching and fund-raising.

Solving those problems is made more difficult because of the nature of the congregation. Expats come and go frequently, and it seems a rule of life that the best people are always moving on elsewhere, while the most tiresome seem to stick around indefinitely. But that mixed-bag congregation makes it all the more compelling. There is a sameness to Anglican congregations in Britain. Moscow's included worshippers from all corners of the Anglosphere (Indians, Americans, Australians and the like). That was to be expected. Less so were the many others: Dutch and Germans, Poles and Finns – not to mention a bunch of Russians. All these people had made a conscious, thought-out decision to go to a church of a different tradition, in a different language.

That is humbling and thought-provoking for someone

brought up to feel that Anglicanism is as unremarkable as bus services or running water. It demonstrated to me Anglicanism's unique inclusivity. Those from the Orthodox tradition were able to feel at home, just as much as those from a Protestant background (one regular attender was a full-time worker for the Salvation Army), or from no religious affiliation at all.

It was when I returned to England that I realized how much more at home I felt in the Church than I had when I left, some fourteen years previously. Living abroad had deepened not only my ties with Anglicanism, but also my knowledge of other Christian denominations. In Russia, I was deeply impressed by the Roman Catholic Church, whose priests' brainy integrity was in sharp contrast to the obscurantism and often dubious practices of much of the Russian Orthodox Church. But I also found much to admire elsewhere in the Eastern tradition. By happy coincidence (or maybe more), I came across a former fellow-student, an American of Ukrainian extraction, who runs a Byzantine-rite Catholic seminary in Ukraine. Although our contact was infrequent, it was inspirational. His seminary – really a university – was a moral lighthouse to a whole region, teaching students everything from classical languages to moral philosophy. Its rigorous standards and loving pastoral care are in sharp contrast to the often corrupt, exploitative and debased system of state-financed university education.

That helped shape my choice of church when I returned to London. Whereas in the past I had been lucky to have one Anglican church to go to, now I had hundreds. I decided to explore a part of the Anglican tradition that I had scarcely encountered in past years. I wanted transcendence, beauty in sound and sight, mystery, reverence and historical continuity; but also a feeling of being part of the widest possible Christian family. So I began going to St Mary's, Bourne Street – probably the most high church of all Anglican churches anywhere.

At first it was rather a shock. I had barely said a Hail Mary in my life, let alone sung the *Salve Regina*. I had never attended Benediction, nor sung plainsong, nor touched a rosary. Some of my friends were surprised. Given that my beloved new wife is Roman Catholic, and that the Anglo-Catholic wing of the Anglican Church is weak, splintered and demoralized, and the whole Church so riven with dispute, they wondered why I didn't take one step further, and join (as one friend kindly put it) 'a proper Catholic Church, rather than a pretend one'.

My answer was that the Church of England is not perfect, but neither are other denominations. It has problems, but so do others. The current rows about sex may get worse, or better, but one does not escape them by moving elsewhere. Equally, whichever course the Church decides to follow, there will be some damage to its ecumenical relations, but the nature of Christian disunity means that there is no single Church that can claim untroubled relations with all other Christians. Leaving the Church you are brought up in is like severing relations with your own family – it may sometimes be necessary, but it should be only the last resort. So long as Anglicanism maintains its inclusivity, tradition and ecumenism, with its ambiguity a witness to humility in the face of the unknowable, I can think of no better spiritual home.

So, for the first time in my adult life, I now feel that my faith and my life are firmly in tune. The Church's job is to provide a framework for modern life, and to fill the gaps. If the secular world is busy, ugly, shallow and selfish, the Church offers peace, rhythm, contemplation, humility, aesthetic riches, history, friendship – all combined in a narrative that makes sense of our actions, hopes and fears. The strands of belief that have passed through my fingers in the past decades have finally knit together. I have never felt more strongly tied to the Church.